be. Again, such a book might well be written in the year 2000.

The other two books are 'twopence coloured', and the colour is laid on thick. They are written with great ability and absolute sincerity, and no one will find either of them dry. They are quite enthralling. Arthur Bryant wrote his book in the autumn of 1939, with the laudable object of encouraging us to see the history of 1919–39 as the average German saw it, and of assuaging the hatred which the on-coming war was almost bound to provoke, that same hatred which, as provoked by the previous war, had, in Bryant's opinion, ruined the prospects of the previous peace settlement. Schwartzchild, a German refugee from Hitler's persecution, wrote in 1942, with the purpose of persuading us that any misplaced leniency, such as had marred the previous peace settlement, would only entail a third war. Bryant's Germany is 'more sinned against than sinning'. Schwartzchild's Germany is the incorrigible enemy of civilization.

It may be that neither of these authors is right. I certainly do not wholly agree with either of them. It is quite certain that they cannot both be right. Clemenceau cannot have been, for example, both the evil genius of the peace conference and the one wise man in an assemblage of sentimentalists and muddlers. But it is by studying the forcible and compelling advocacy of both books, and by checking them against each other and against the cool impartiality of such a book as Gathorne-Hardy's, that the reader may come to realize something of the horrid complexity of the subject on which I have now to embark.

BETWEEN THE WARS

HOME STUDY BOOKS
General Editor: B. Ifor Evans

BETWEEN THE WARS

by

D. C. SOMERVELL

METHUEN & CO. LTD., LONDON
36 Essex Street, Strand, W.C.2

HOME STUDY BOOKS
General Editor: B. Ifor Evans

BETWEEN THE WARS

by

D. C. SOMERVELL

METHUEN & CO. LTD., LONDON
36 Essex Street, Strand, W.C.2

First published in 1948

CATALOGUE NO. 4444/U

THIS BOOK IS PRODUCED IN
COMPLETE CONFORMITY WITH THE
AUTHORIZED ECONOMY STANDARDS

PRINTED IN GREAT BRITAIN

PREFACE

THIS book is not a history of things in general that happened between the two wars: an attempt to provide this would result in an overcrowded and miscellaneous picture. It is an attempt to assemble the main facts providing evidence for an answer to the question, why was the first great war followed by another?

Dozens and scores of books have been written on the history of the period 'between the wars'. A few of these are noted at the end of this volume. I wish here to say a few words about three of them, namely *A Short History of International Relations, 1920–1939* by G. M. Gathorne-Hardy, *Unfinished Victory* by Arthur Bryant, and *World in Trance* by Leopold Schwartzchild.

Historical works have been classified as 'penny plain' and 'twopence coloured'. Gathorne-Hardy's book, published on behalf of the Royal Institute of International Affairs, is an excellent example of the former variety. It offers a careful and conscientiously unbiassed record of events, from which the reader may draw what conclusions he can. If it is a trifle dry, its dryness is a virtue. One feels that, within the limits which the author sets himself, it can be trusted. It was written by an Englishman, for the most part in 1934 and completed in 1940, but one feels that a similar book might have been written by a Frenchman or a German gifted with an equal power of detachment—if any such there be. Again, such a book might well be written in the year 2000.

The other two books are 'twopence coloured', and the colour is laid on thick. They are written with great ability and absolute sincerity, and no one will find either of them dry. They are quite enthralling. Arthur Bryant wrote his book in the autumn of 1939, with the laudable object of encouraging us to see the history of 1919–39 as the average German saw it, and of assuaging the hatred which the on-coming war was almost bound to provoke, that same hatred which, as provoked by the previous war, had, in Bryant's opinion, ruined the prospects of the previous peace settlement. Schwartzchild, a German refugee from Hitler's persecution, wrote in 1942, with the purpose of persuading us that any misplaced leniency, such as had marred the previous peace settlement, would only entail a third war. Bryant's Germany is 'more sinned against than sinning'. Schwartzchild's Germany is the incorrigible enemy of civilization.

It may be that neither of these authors is right. I certainly do not wholly agree with either of them. It is quite certain that they cannot both be right. Clemenceau cannot have been, for example, both the evil genius of the peace conference and the one wise man in an assemblage of sentimentalists and muddlers. But it is by studying the forcible and compelling advocacy of both books, and by checking them against each other and against the cool impartiality of such a book as Gathorne-Hardy's, that the reader may come to realize something of the horrid complexity of the subject on which I have now to embark.

I have written on these matters before, and have occasionally borrowed, with little or no alteration, paragraphs from two of my previous books, a short text-book entitled *Europe 1871–1939*, and a more detailed and ambitious work entitled *A History of the Reign of George V*.

I am reading these proofs in the early summer of 1946, but the book was written in the early summer of 1945, at the German final collapse and surrender. I was thus, perhaps fortunately, spared the temptation to draw analogies, between the post-war confusions of 1919 and those of today.

D.C.S.

CONTENTS

I
PARIS

THIS book might well have been called 'The History of a Failure'. The period which it covers begins with the conclusion of a four years' world war which, whatever its original causes, had become, in the minds of the statesmen and peoples of at least some of the principal belligerents on what proved the victorious side, a 'war to end war'. The victory was complete beyond all expectation; and yet, within twenty-one years, another war of almost exactly the same kind had begun.

People often think and speak and write as if this failure were not only deplorable but extraordinary, and not to be expected. They seem to assume that there must have been not only very great villains at work on one side, but also very great fools at work on the other to produce such a result. But surely that must not be assumed. *Humanum est errare*: it is the nature of man to make mistakes, and mistakes on great issues are great mistakes. The only periods of history in which there are no great failures are the ignoble periods in which no great things were attempted. In our period of twenty-one years the statesmen of our Western society set out to do one of the most difficult things ever attempted; they set out to eradicate a habit of the human race which was as old as our oldest historical records, and no doubt much older, namely the habit of settling

1

disputes by fighting. Moreover, they undertook thi task at a time when its successful accomplishment had become unusually difficult, and that for two reasons. On the one hand the discoveries of science had placed at the disposal of the art of war all kinds of new and fascinating instruments of destruction, such as would encourage an aggressor to assume that this time at any rate he could not fail. On the other hand, the whole world had become democratic; the policy of statesmen was, as never before, at the mercy of ignorant and emotional multitudes. The ancient institution of international war had been reinforced by two modern forces, which Arnold Toynbee calls 'the drive of industrialism' and 'the drive of democracy'.[1] At the same time, though the whole world had become democratic in sentiment, no satisfactory political machinery had been—or perhaps ever can be—discovered through which an ignorant democracy can discover a rational will, and impose it on its rulers.

Our own well-tried parliamentary system has proved applicable only in a democracy which has arrived at years of discretion. It has proved workable in English-speaking countries and in a few small states of north-western Europe; hardly anywhere else. Elsewhere we find, during this period, corrupt and inefficient parliamentary democracies, as in France, or pseudo-democratic dictatorships.

None the less it is natural that the victims of the Second World War should scan the records of the inter-war period in search not only of the villains— some of these are easily identified—but also of the fools whose folly made possible this terrible failure.

[1] *A Study of History*, by A. J. Toynbee, Vol. IV, pp. 141–156.

Two groups in particular have been singled out and exposed to such charges of folly. One group is the group of the 'appeasers' who, when once Hitler had entered on the course which led straight to the Second World War, persisted in hoping for the best and refrained from 'nipping' him 'in the bud'. The other group is that of the authors of the peace treaties of 1919 who, it is alleged, gave the great post-war experiment a thoroughly bad start. We shall reach the appeasers in a later chapter of this book. At present our concern is with the men of 1919 and their work.

Few episodes in history present a broader target to the shafts of criticism than the Paris Peace Conference, but it is a strange misunderstanding of history to suggest that the peace treaties, in themselves, gave the post-war experiment a bad start—as though 'everything in the garden was lovely' until the peace treaties entered it, like Satan entering the Garden of Eden. That experiment had been given a bad start in any case—by the four years of war, which had left a world full of such international hatreds as had never been known before, the legacy of a war which had engaged the energies and wounded the hearts of men and women of all classes to a degree unprecedented in human history. It is wishful thinking to suppose that war is a surgical operation, and that the overthrow of a Kaiser or a Hitler is comparable with the neat excision of an appendix. War is a disease, and its worst damages are inflicted on the minds of the peoples involved— the longing for revenge, easily gratified at once in the case of the victors, slowly smouldering and biding its time in the case of the vanquished. The peace treaties, immense masses of detailed work, hurried through by tired and quarrelsome statesmen, each of them with one eye continually distracted towards his own turbulent and hysterical democracy at home—these treaties were a war product and inevitably bore the stamp of the war from which they emerged, and of the war-fever in which they were composed.

Only by a miracle could the treaties have been good treaties, but their critics in large measure answer one another. One school of thought, certainly the prevalent school of thought in English-speaking countries before the rise of Hitler, held that the treaties were too severe to the defeated countries. These critics found their villain in Clemenceau, the French prime minister and the President of the Peace Conference. Clemenceau held that the Germans were brutes and always would be brutes, and that the only thing to do with them was to strap them down—not for ever, only because that would prove impossible, but at any rate for as long as possible. This seemed a very deplorable point of view to liberal-minded Englishmen and Americans of the pre-Hitler period. We declared that Clemenceau was merely another Bismarck on the other side of the Rhine, and indeed these two supermen had many points in common. Both were hard-headed realists with first-class brains and abominable tempers, which they controlled or released with diplomatic adroitness. Yet some years before 1939 many liberal critics began to wonder if Clemenceau had not been right after all.

Other critics, more especially in France, attacked the treaties from the first on the ground that they were not sufficiently severe to the beaten enemy. Certainly many of the severer clauses were never really enforced, because their enforcement would have meant the occupation of Germany, and the abandonment of the conception of Germany as still a sovereign independent state, a conception on which the treaty was based. It would have meant in fact a renewal of war. Thus Germany never carried out even in the letter, much less in the spirit, the drastic disarmament clauses of the treaty.

Perhaps one can combine what is true and reject what is false in both these schools of criticism, and say that the Treaty of Versailles inflicted on Germany too much insult and too little injury. The humiliation of defeat was thoroughly rubbed in, but once the country had recovered from its wounds—wounds inflicted less by the treaty than by the catastrophe of the war—it was fully able to prepare its revenge, as events showed.

Only by a miracle, as we have said, could the treaties of 1919 have been good treaties. But one of the most singular features of the winter of 1918–19 was that millions of people confidently expected the miracle, and acclaimed the forthcoming miracle-worker—President Wilson. These optimists were, perhaps, most numerous in the British Isles. They were certainly less numerous in America, where the President's weaknesses were well known, but there were plenty of them there also, and in Germany and Italy; fewer in France, and fewest of all in Paris where, by an unfortunate but inevitable decision— inevitable since France, the principal martyr of the war wished it to be so—the Peace Conference was to be held.

Woodrow Wilson, an American professor of history and political science, whom the lottery of American politics had elevated to the Presidency of the United States in 1912, stood for certain principles very easy to state in general terms and very difficult to apply to the indescribable complexities of the European situation: a peace based on justice to victors and vanquished alike; self-determination of nationalities, or frontiers drawn in accordance with the wishes of populations; the acceptance of a Covenant abolishing war, and the institution of a League of Nations for the settlement of international disputes. There was nothing new about this political idealism. What was new was the fact that it was explicitly accepted as a programme of action by the ruler of the most powerful community in the world, the one great power which, having entered the war only in its later stages, and having been actively engaged in it only during its last few months, emerged from it with its resources fully mobilized and scarcely at all impaired. If Europe could have believed that America would support, and continue for a generation to support, a Wilsonian peace with all the resources at its disposal, it is just conceivable that Europe might have been persuaded to accept a Wilsonian settlement. Unfortunately Europe had very little reason for believing this, and very valid reasons for believing the exact opposite, namely that, whatever Wilson might say or do in Paris, America would withdraw as quickly as possible into her traditional isolation and leave Europe to stew in her own juice. That being so, the realists of Continental politics, from Clemenceau downwards to the representatives of the most obscure and primitive of the submerged nationalities which sprang up amidst the ruins of derelict empires and demanded independence, determined to 'make hay while the sun shone', and obtain for themselves all that they could get at the expense of their immediate neighbours and enemies.

Indeed, if the President's task was insuperably difficult, he was in any case ill-equipped to accomplish it. He was, by European standards, an unskilful politician, unaccustomed to the rough and tumble of hard bargaining with his political equals. Though he brought with him from America an admirable staff of experts, he made little use of them, and he had a curious capacity for shutting his eyes to unpleasant facts. An extraordinary illustration of this was furnished by some remarks which he addressed to the American delegation while they were crossing the Atlantic on their way to Paris. He told them that 'these people', meaning the Allied statesmen, Clemenceau, Lloyd George, and others, did not really represent their democracies, whereas he, Wilson, did. But the facts, as his hearers must have realized if their critical faculties were awake, were the exact opposite. Lloyd George had just held a general election, which had given him the largest majority ever yet accorded to a British statesman. Clemenceau had just obtained a five to one vote of confidence in the French chamber of deputies. Wilson, appealing for a Democratic party majority in the 'mid-term' elections of November 1918, had suffered a severe defeat.[1] If the tenure of the American Presidency

---

[1] Under the American constitution Congressional elections are held every two years, both at the time of a Presidential election and midway between such elections.

had been regulated by the same rule as the tenure of the British Prime Ministership, Wilson would have already ceased to be President. He had indeed secured his re-election in 1916 by the very narrowest of majorities.

The elements of the Wilsonian programme had been tabulated as early as January 1918 in the famous Fourteen Points (see Appendix I), and this statement had become by the time of the Peace Conference something much more than a collection of pious opinions. When, in October 1918, the German Government realized that defeat was inevitable, Prince Max of Baden, the last Chancellor of the Imperial régime, addressed a dispatch to Wilson asking him to arrange an armistice between Germany and her enemies. Wilson replied, asking the Chancellor if his government accepted his statement of peace terms contained in the Fourteen Points, and two other less detailed, but in some respects more sweeping, pronouncements (the Four Principles and the Five Particulars). Prince Max replied in the affirmative, and he afterwards told the world in his memoirs that neither he nor the German High Command had any clear idea at the time what drastic and specific penalties the Points themselves imposed upon Germany. They imagined that they were an assortment of vague 'ideals' out of which they could extract useful arguments for their own advantage.

Wilson then turned to the Allied governments and addressed to them the same question. The British Government objected to the second of the Fourteen Points, a vague statement about 'the freedom of the seas', and asked for the addition of a further 'Point', that the Allies should be entitled to exact from

Germany reparations (repayment) for all damage done 'to the civilian population of the Allies on land, at sea, and from the air'. This would include payment for the destruction of towns by bombardment and of ships, other than naval vessels, by submarines.

When the European Allies found themselves invited to accept Wilson's Points as a basis for the future peace settlement they had sought from Colonel House, Wilson's representative in Paris, an interpretation of the more obscure passages, and the general effect of the Colonel's interpretations was to reduce the more alarming 'Points' to harmlessness. For example, Point 3 might seem to mean the establishment of universal free trade; but according to House it was not intended to forbid any tariffs so long as they were applied against all foreign countries alike. In Point 4, dealing with disarmament, House interpreted the phrase 'domestic safety' to mean self-defence. Point 5, dealing with colonial claims, did not mean (as the Germans very naturally supposed) that they were to have a fair share— whatever that might be—of colonial territory, but only that whatever nations received ex-enemy colonial territories was to be responsible for them to the League of Nations. Point 1 did not mean that diplomatic negotiations should henceforth be conducted in public (which would be absurd, though that is what the Point seems to say), but simply that, when negotiations had resulted in treaties, such treaties should be published. The Allied governments could therefore claim that what they had accepted was the House version of the Points, but the Germans were never informed of this version, either before or after the armistice.

It was, of course, extremely unwise and unfortunate that the Allied governments allowed themselves, under pressure from Wilson and House, to be entangled in a pre-armistice pledge to construct the peace treaties in accordance with the Points, for they were militarily in a position to demand unconditional surrender. The Points were general statements, capable of a variety of interpretations; suitable enough in a platform speech, which was their original context, but unsuitable for use as terms governing a bargain between hostile nations. Mr. Harold Nicolson, who himself played a part in the making of the treaties, goes so far as to say that the peace treaties violated no less than nineteen of the twenty-three 'Points, Principles and Particulars'. Thus the Germans were afterwards entitled to make the effective debating point that the war, which had begun with the tearing up of one scrap of paper, ended with the tearing up of another.[1] None the less, the pre-armistice acceptance of the Points by the Allies placed Wilson in a strong position, and he made curiously little use of his advantage. It seems as though, caught in the swirl and torrent of crabbed details and hard facts, Wilson lost interest in all his Points except the last one, the League of Nations. The treaties, he came to realize, were bound to be bad; but he persuaded himself that if the League of Nations Covenant were thrust into the treaties as an integral part of the settlement, it would provide

---

[1] In answer to this another equally good debating point has been made, namely that there never was any pledge *to Germany* that the treaty would accord with the Points. Germany was asked if she accepted the Points and replied in the affirmative. The Allies and the American government agreed *as between themselves* to respect the terms of the Points.

an effective instrument for their revision when the passions of war had cooled down.

Innumerable books have been written about the Peace Conference. The most illuminating known to me is *Peacemaking 1919* by Harold Nicolson, who as a young foreign office official was himself a member of the British delegation. The first half of the book contains his reflections written fourteen years afterwards, sufficiently early to be unaffected by the rise of the Nazi power. The second part contains his journal, written day by day from January to June 1919, and concluding with the signature of the Treaty of Versailles by the German delegates. In this we see a young professional diplomatist entering on his duties an enthusiastic devotee of Wilsonian idealism. As the months pass he becomes rapidly disillusioned and disgusted with the sordid trafficking of the committees it is his duty to attend, realizing at the same time that his prophet is proving entirely unable to give substance to the hopes he has encouraged. He ends in weariness and despair. 'One writes the sentence: "It was a period of unremitting strain." The sedative notes of such a sentence, as applied to the scurrying cacophony of the Peace Conference, force one to smile. Only through the medium of a sound-film could any accurate impression, that sense of a riot in a parrot house, be conveyed.'[1] Nicolson considers that the fundamental error of the Conference was that, astonishing as it must seem, it never adopted any thought-out programme of procedure. The French had framed a programme, but Wilson rejected it without offering

[1] Nicolson op. cit., p. 152. The quotation is not from the Journal but from the first part of the book.

an alternative of his own. As for Lloyd George, he was by nature a brilliant improvisor and opportunist, and the qualities that had made him a great war minister proved a disqualification after the fighting was over. Nicolson also warns his readers against the popular simplification which regards the Conference as a duel between Wilson and Clemenceau with Lloyd George oscillating from one side to the other. The issues were nothing like so clear cut. From first to last it was a case of all against all, a jumble and a scramble, conducted in a world of ever-increasing chaos, driven on by an urgent sense that a quick peace would be better than a good peace, even if one admitted the improbable supposition that a good peace could be secured by delay. Many of the most important clauses of the treaties were hurried improvisations substituted at the last minute for something else.

The most extraordinary illustration of the haphazard character of the proceedings was the fact that the peace treaties were not, like all previous settlements of the kind, negotiated with the enemy states, but were negotiated by the Allies with each other, and imposed upon the enemy states by simple dictation after a brief exchange of arguments in writing. The original idea seems to have been that the Conference should draft preliminary treaties to be enforced on the enemy states, and then convert itself into a Peace Congress by inviting the representatives of these states to a round table discussion of the more difficult and detailed issues and the formulation of final treaties. This had been the procedure adopted after the Napoleonic wars, when a preliminary Treaty of Paris was followed by a Congress of Vienna.

The precedent illustrated, no doubt, the dangers of such a procedure, for at Vienna the ingenious Talleyrand had succeeded in splitting the ex-enemies of France, and making France the ally of Britain and Austria against the claims of Russia and Prussia. His work was only spoilt by the insensate return of Napoleon from Elba. There was, so far as we know, no German of the calibre of Talleyrand available in 1919, but imagination boggles at the conception of a German Talleyrand allying himself with Wilson and Lloyd George against Clemenceau and the Italians (Orlando and Sonnino), only to see his card-castle collapsed by the return of the ex-Kaiser from his place of exile at Doorn on the Zuyder Zee.

What actually happened was that more and more material got pushed into the supposed preliminary treaty until it became in fact the one and only treaty and the idea of a Congress including the representatives of the ex-enemy states was abandoned. These second thoughts, strange as it may seem, secured the obstinate support of Wilson, who in this point was on the same side as Clemenceau. Wilson had worked himself into a thoroughly false position. He was compelled to pretend that the treaty, which he would have to recommend to the acceptance of the American Senate, was in accordance with his Fourteen Points' policy. A conference with ex-enemy delegates would inevitably expose this pretence, and he was not prepared to face such exposure. There can be no doubt that the dictation of the peace terms to the ex-enemy states, without any round table discussions, was a disaster of the first magnitude. The treaties would almost certainly have been improved as a result of such discussions, but that is not the main

point. The *Diktat*, as the Germans always called it,
confirmed and perpetuated the division of Europe
into victors and vanquished, and carried it over into
the inter-war period. This schism was, of course,
deepened when France refused to allow the admission
of the ex-enemy states to membership of the League
of Nations.

Early in May the completed treaty was handed to
German delegates summoned to receive it, and on
28 June other German delegates, obscure envoys of
the newly constituted Weimar Republic, Müller and
Bell, were conducted to the Hall of Mirrors in the
Palace of Versailles to affix their signatures to the
Diktat. Here is Harold Nicolson's description of this
horrid event, written at the time.

'. . . The Gardes Republicains at the doorway
flash their swords into their scabbards with a loud
click. "*Faites entrer les Allemands,*" says Clemenceau in the ensuing silence. . . . Through the door
at the end appear two huissiers with silver chains.
They march in single file. After them come four
officers of France, Great Britain, America, and
Italy. And then, isolated and pitiable, the two
German delegates. Dr. Müller, Dr. Bell. The
silence is terrifying. Their feet upon a strip of
parquet between the carpets echo hollow and
duplicate. They keep their eyes fixed away from
those two thousand staring eyes, fixed upon the
ceiling. They are deathly pale. They do not appear
as representatives of a brutal militarism. The one
is thin and pink-eyelidded: the second fiddle in a
Brunswick orchestra. The other is moon-faced and
suffering: a privat-dozent. It is most painful.

'They are conducted to their chairs. Clemenceau at once breaks the silence. "*Messieurs*," he rasps, "*le séance est ouverte*." He adds a few ill-chosen words . . . The Germans are led to the little table on which the Treaty is expanded. There is general tension. They sign. There is general relaxation . . . [After this all the Allied representatives sign the treaty] . . . There is a final hush. "*La séance est levée*" rasped Clemenceau. Not a word more or less. We kept our seats while the German delegates were conducted like prisoners from the dock, their eyes fixed upon some distant spot on the horizon.

'We still kept our seats to allow the Big Five to pass down the aisle. Wilson, Lloyd George, the Dominions, others. Finally Clemenceau, with his rolling satirical gait. Painlevé, who was sitting one off me, rose to greet him. He stretched out both his hands and grasped his right glove. He congratulated him. "*Oui*," says Clemenceau, "*c'est une belle journée*." There were tears in his bleary eyes.

'Marie Murat was near me and had overheard. "*En êtes vous sûre?*" I ask her. "*Pas du tout*", she answers, being a woman of intelligence.'

THE TREATY OF VERSAILLES

The treaties dictated by the Paris Conference were named after various places in the neighbourhood, the German treaty being called the Treaty of Versailles. It was followed by the Treaty of Saint-Germains with Austria, the Treaty of Trianon with Hungary, the Treaty of Neuilly with Bulgaria, and finally, in 1920, the Treaty of Sèvres with Turkey. The naming of this last treaty proved most appropriate, for Sèvres is known to the world for its historic porcelain factory, and the Treaty of Sèvres was, a few years later, smashed to smithereens by the resurgent Turkey of Mustapha Kemal, and another and very different treaty had to be negotiated at Lausanne to replace it in 1923. At present we are concerned only with the German treaty.

As regards territory, Germany lost Alsace and Lorraine, taken from France in 1871, and now restored to her. That was a foregone conclusion. France also obtained for fifteen years the coalfield of the Saar valley, to the north of Lorraine, as compensation for the destruction of her collieries in the war zone of northern France. At the end of fifteen years the inhabitants of the Saar valley were to vote as to their future destiny, and as they were nearly all German it was likely that they would vote for re-inclusion in Germany. This was what happened, in 1935, and though it was in no respect due to the establishment of the Nazi régime two years earlier, it helped to increase the prestige of the Nazi government. Some small and unimportant strips of German territory were also given to Belgium, on the ground that Belgians predominated among their inhabitants.

France wanted to annex all German territory up to the Rhine, or at any rate to enforce its complete separation from the rest of Germany, such separation to be secured, if necessary, by the permanent establishment of French or Allied garrisons within the territory. Only so, argued Foch, could France be given a secure frontier against her enemy. Clemenceau refused to put forward this claim, because he knew that he could not sustain it against the opposition of Britain and America. The inclusion within France or the enforced separation from the rest of Germany of a territory inhabited by over 8,000,000 Germans would have been too glaring a breach of the principle of self-determination. The result for Clemenceau was that he was defeated when, in the following year, he sought to crown his illustrious career by securing the Presidency of the French Republic.

Denmark had remained neutral throughout the war, but she profited by an application of the principles of the victorious belligerents. The Duchy of Schleswig had been attached to the Danish crown for four hundred years previous to 1864, when it was annexed by Prussia after the first of Bismarck's wars. A plebiscite was now held in the Duchy as a result of which the northern part of it was restored to Denmark.

The eastern frontier of Germany presented a far more difficult problem, for all the way down from the Baltic to Czechoslovakia Germans and Poles, who hated one another, were inextricably intermingled. On the Baltic coast eastwards from the Vistula was a German population in East Prussia, which had been ruled by the Hohenzollerns of Berlin since 1619, whereas to the west of the Vistula, apart from the mainly German port of Danzig, was a province with a preponderantly Polish population. On the principle of self-determination, therefore, East Prussia remained German, but was separated from the rest of Germany by a 'Polish corridor' to the sea, thus undoing the work of Frederick the Great of Prussia, who had annexed this province of

West Prussia in the 'first partition of Poland', in 1772. The German city of Danzig was Poland's neutral outlet to the sea. It was, therefore, taken from Germany and placed under the control of a Commissioner appointed by the League of Nations. Its municipal government was left to the German population, but the harbour was placed in Polish control, an arrangement which never worked smoothly and proved, twenty years later, the *casus belli* of the second great war. Farther south the German province of Posen (Poznan) was taken from Germany, and, farther south again, the important industrial area of Upper Silesia, after a plebiscite which showed the two races to be so intermingled that no settlement could give satisfaction to both parties, was divided between Poland and Germany. The holding of this plebiscite was one of the few concessions that the Germans extorted from the Peace Conference after the treaty had been handed to them and before its signature. In the original draft the whole of Upper Silesia had been allocated to Poland.

One cannot say that any better or fairer settlement of the Polish-German frontier problem was possible, but it was obvious from the first that, if and when the power of Germany revived, this frontier would, unless by that time the Germans and the Poles had become friendly with one another, become one of the storm centres of Europe.

So much for the territory lost by Germany in Europe. It meant the loss of about 5,000,000 of her population and of two very important industrial districts, part of Upper Silesia and the iron mines of Lorraine; also, temporarily, the coal of the Saar valley. Yet on the whole, except for the temporary cession of the Saar valley and the special case of Danzig, these changes were in accordance with the will of the majority of the inhabitants.

But a paring down of German frontiers would be of little value to any but the 5,000,000 people emancipated from her rule if Germany remained free to attack her neighbours when she felt disposed. At the end of the Conference, America would go home across the Atlantic, and England would go home across the Channel, pleasantly conscious of the fact that the German fleet was at the bottom of Scapa Flow, where the surrendered ships had been scuttled by their own crews. Both the English-speaking powers were already recklessly demobilizing their armies. But 40,000,000 Frenchmen would remain confronting 70,000,000 Germans. How was France to achieve security? Wilson, who had found the idea of a war-time truce between the Republican and Democratic parties of his own country unthinkable, had said that the French and the Germans must let bygones be bygones and make friends, but the French did not deem this feasible. Their demand for a Rhine frontier from Holland to Alsace had been refused. Instead, the Allies made two offers with which France had to be content. All German territory west of the Rhine and a thirty-mile strip to the east of it was to be occupied by Allied troops for a limited period, one-third being evacuated in five years, another in ten, and the remainder in fifteen years. However, these evacuations were not to be made unless Germany fulfilled the obligations imposed on her by the treaty. After the withdrawal of the Allied troops this Rhineland area was to be

permanently demilitarized; though under complete
German sovereignty in other respects, Germany was
not to keep any troops or make any fortifications
within it. This might well be regarded as some
security, especially as it seemed unlikely that
Germany would ever be able to pay the stupendous
bill of reparations which was being assessed against
her. The danger was that nations other than France
might tire of keeping an indefinitely prolonged watch
on the Rhine, and that, when the Allied garrisons
withdrew and the passions of war died down, other
nations besides Germany, perhaps all nations other
than Germany's immediate neighbours, might feel it
unreasonable that Germany should not be entitled
to make what use she pleased of her own territory.
In other words, Germany would send her armies into
her own Rhineland province, and public opinion
outside France, Poland, and Czechoslovakia would
feel that, after all, she was morally entitled to do so.
This is exactly what happened in 1936.

The other security offered to France was a joint
Anglo-American undertaking to come to her immediate assistance if attacked. Unfortunately this
instrument of security disappeared when, in 1920,
the American Senate rejected the Versailles Treaty,
for the British guarantee, being a joint guarantee
with America, lapsed at the same time.

It remained to be seen whether any security for
France could be got by way of disarmament.
Wilson's ideal, shared by many in England, was that
ultimately there should be disarmament all round,
but that was clearly a matter for consideration at
some future date. It was one of the tasks to be
entrusted to the League of Nations. At present it

must suffice to disarm Germany. Conscription in Germany was henceforth forbidden, and the German army limited to a force of 100,000 long-service troops, a number deemed sufficient for the maintenance of internal order. The German navy was to be limited to six battleships, with certain minor craft. There were to be no submarines, and no air force. Allied officials were to supervise the enforcement of these measures.

So long as Germany was disarmed France certainly would enjoy security, and she further strengthened her position by alliances with Germany's new eastern neighbours, Poland and Czechoslovakia. The 'post-war' period, in the proper sense of the term, is the period during which Germany continued to be disarmed and France to dominate western Europe. But it could not continue for ever. Either general disarmament, vaguely foreshadowed in the treaty, would follow, or else German rearmament. When the time came, in the early 'thirties, France refused the former course and Germany adopted the latter.

Why did France block all genuine schemes for disarmament? The answer, reduced to fundamentals, is that there were only 40,000,000 Frenchmen and over 70,000,000 Germans. When France and Germany are placed on an equality France, unless she is absolutely secure of the immediate support of a very powerful ally, is at the mercy of Germany.

One could make a long list of the further disabilities imposed on Germany. She was deprived of all her overseas possessions, and all state property in these colonies was confiscated. Her rights of trade by pre-war treaties with China, Morocco, Equatorial Africa, etc. were abolished. The Kiel Canal was neutralized, and the navigation of the Rhine entrusted to an international commission. And, finally, there was reparations.

This was an extremely difficult problem, and for its mishandling by the Conference British statesmanship must bear a large share of the blame. Having no territorial claims, apart from the claim to a share of the German colonies, which aroused little interest in Britain, though much in Australia and South Africa, the British electorate concentrated with a most unfortunate enthusiasm on the payment of its financial claims, oblivious of the fact that many economists of high repute held that such claims could not be paid from one nation to another without doing as much damage to the receiver as to the debtor. If, for example, German industry replaced the British ships sunk by U-boats, what would become of the British shipbuilding industry? In the deplorable election campaign launched by Lloyd George's coalition government immediately after the armistice, not even the hanging of the Kaiser and the immediate abolition of conscription excited such passionate and frantic interest as the financial damages to be exacted from the beaten enemy. Under pressure from his audiences Lloyd George committed himself to three principles: first, we had an absolute right to demand the whole cost of the war; second, we proposed to demand it; third, a committee appointed by the Cabinet and containing the Governor of the Bank of England believed it could be done. Lloyd George must have known that this was nonsense, and he seems to have forgotten that in the pre-armistice correspondence his government had claimed the right to reparations for damage to *civilian* property and had thereby presumably disclaimed any intention of claiming reparations for anything else.

When the reparations question came to be discussed at the Peace Conference, Mr. Keynes, a Cambridge economist employed as a financial expert by the British delegation, resigned his position in disgust and published a blasting criticism of the reparations clauses of the treaty entitled *The Economic Consequences of the Peace*, a book which did more than anything else to discredit the peace settlement in the eyes not only of the British public, but in the eyes of the German and American publics as well; a fact in many ways unfortunate for the stability of the post-war world which had, for better or worse, to take the peace treaties as its foundation, since there was no other.

We will not entangle ourselves in the details of this distressing subject. Keynes estimated that the reparation claims valid under the armistice terms might be estimated at £3,000,000,000, a figure which Germany might just conceivably have been able to pay off in the course of the next fifty years, allowing 5 per cent interest on the debt. The Conference added other claims, justifying them by means of the once celebrated 'war guilt clause'. 'The Allied and associated governments affirm and Germany accepts the responsibility of Germany and her Allies for causing *all*[1] the loss and damage to which the Allied and associated governments and their nationals have been subjected as a consequence of the war imposed on them by the aggression of Germany and her Allies.' The reparation claims

[1] Italics mine.

thus added to the armistice claims much more than doubled their financial dimensions. Finally, no figure was named in the treaty, and the whole problem was handed over to a Reparations Commission to be appointed in due course. This was, so far as it went, a wise move. At some future date, when sanity was restored, the Reparations Commission might do for the reparations demand what President Wilson hoped the League of Nations would do for the other more extravagant features of the treaty.

Such were some of the principal features of the Treaty of Versailles. It has few admirers, but it is possible to blame it overmuch, and in particular to exaggerate both its departures from the Fourteen Points and its share of the responsibility for the misfortunes of the next twenty years. German propaganda represented it as a kind of torture chamber, from which Germany could only escape by fighting another round of the battle with her enemies; but that, like most German propaganda, is all nonsense. The principal engine of torture in this treaty was the reparations demand and, taking one thing with another, reparations were never paid! As will be seen when we are forced to return to the subject, Germany in the period 1920–31 borrowed (and never repaid) much more from investors in America and elsewhere than she ever paid out in reparations; and after 1931, *before* the rise of Hitler, reparation payments were suspended once for all. As for the war-guilt clause, about which German propaganda made such a fuss, it may have been an insult; it may even have been a deserved insult; but it was not an injury. There were also clauses concerning the punishment of war criminals, but this, which loomed so large in 1919, came to almost nothing. In the end a dozen obscure military sadists were prosecuted by the Allies in Germany, before German judges. Six were sentenced to most inadequate penalties and six were acquitted.

Perhaps we are better able now, when another German war settlement is in immediate prospect, than were the writers of the inter-war period to estimate just where the Treaty of Versailles was inadequate to its opportunity. It may be regarded as an untenable 'half-way house' between the peace treaties of past ages and the post-war fundamental reorganization to which we, not very hopefully perhaps, now look forward. Old wars were fought with limited resources for limited objectives, seldom ended in overwhelming victory, were followed by limited changes, and left but little legacy of hatred and malice behind them. Both the wars and the treaties were common form, and those who fought and ran away would live to fight another day. The 1914–18 war was the first total war, ending in overwhelming victory, and demanding a radical solution which would render total war henceforth impossible. Yet the Versailles Treaty is, in comparison with the 'new-order war' which it followed, an old-order affair. 'The mixture as before' is administered to the enemy state, even though the dose was an unprecedently strong one. The conception of the enemy as a sovereign state remained intact. The fault of the Versailles Treaty is the same as the fault of the constitution of the League of Nations, to which we shall come in the last section of this chapter. The old-world conception of independent sovereign states was not transcended. And why not?—because not one person in a thousand anywhere in the world wished it to be.

And the statesmen were only a very little wiser than the millions they represented? Of course. If they had been too much wiser they would not have been statesmen; they would have been obscure journalists of left-wing periodicals. Then are such journalists greater men than statesmen? Assuredly not. It takes a great deal of human quality to make a Lloyd George or a Clemenceau, and comparatively little to make a left-wing journalist. In other words, it is very easy to have a good idea and to write about it, but it is very hard to quicken the pace of the human mass as it moves, if it does move, towards the millennium, and this, nothing less, is the arduous task to which any statesmanship worthy of the name is dedicated.

THE OTHER TREATIES

The disruption of the old Habsburg Empire, the Dual Monarchy of Austria-Hungary, was not the work of the Conference. It had been already accomplished in the last weeks of the war and the interval between the armistice and the treaties. During the war we were often invited to study ethnic maps of this Empire, showing the distribution of its various national groups, Austrian Germans, Magyars (Hungarians), Czechs and Slovaks, Poles and Ruthenians, Rumanians, Serbs, Croats and Slovenes, Italians. These maps, if at all accurate, showed various mottled and criss-cross areas where the nationalities overlapped. The work of the various committees appointed by the Peace Conference was to draw frontiers through these doubtful regions.

In the result the frontiers were somewhat less than fair to the ex-enemy nationalities. Germans and Magyars who had dominated the policy of the old Empire and provoked the war by the ultimatum following the Sarajevo murder, got rather less territory than perhaps they deserved, not because the umpires cherished any animosity against these peoples, for the British and American representatives certainly did not do so, as because their case was, like the German case, unrepresented, whereas the representatives of all the rest were present and volubly insistent. There were the Italians, Orlando and Sonnino, who, unlike President Wilson, succeeded in being worthy of their ideal, which was not perhaps very difficult, for it had been expressed by one of them in the words 'sacro egoismo'. There was the industrious and persuasive Beneš from Czechoslovakia, the repulsive Bratianu from Rumania, the steadfast Trumbic from 'the S.C.S.', for the name Jugoslavia (Southern Slavland) had not yet become current, and this enlargement of the savage little kingdom of Serbia was known as the kingdom of the Serbs, Croats, and Slovenes. There was also Paderewski, once the most famous pianist in the world, and now only Prime Minister of Poland ('What a come down!' said Clemenceau when he heard about it); but Paderewski still looked more like an artist than a statesman, and forcibly reminded Mr. Nicolson of Algernon Charles Swinburne. Thus when the Czech and the S.C.S. committees compared notes and discovered how little their combined efforts had left of Hungary, they were somewhat astonished and dismayed; for there had been no Hungarian committee to look at the matter from the other side.

All these new or enlarged states contained more or less considerable minorities, Sudeten Germans in Czechoslovakia, for example, and Magyars in the Transylvanian province of the enlarged Rumania. Also it was by no means certain how well or how badly the kindred but distinct resurgent groups who had combined to form the new states would get on together, the civilized and industrial Czechs with the primitive Slovaks, for example, or the Catholic and fairly civilized Croats and Slovenes, long ruled from Vienna, with the Orthodox and sturdy Serbs, who had known no more civilizing influences than the Turks, the Magyars and the alternations of their own rival and bloodstained dynasties.

The historic capital of Vienna, once the centre of a great empire, found itself the capital of a forlorn 'tadpole' republic, with a narrow tail wandering westwards through villages and charming mountain scenery to the Swiss frontier. Austria asked to be allowed to unite herself with Germany, and this was forbidden, a flagrant defiance of the principle of self-determination, no doubt; but if the demand had been accepted Czechoslovakia would have been in the uncomfortable position of having Germany on three sides of her Czech province, the Bohemia of pre-war maps. The best hope for Austria, failing union with Germany, was the establishment of something approaching free trade relations with the 'succession states', as they were called, of the old Habsburg Empire. Indeed that Empire, however indefensible and doomed on nationalistic grounds, had served the middle Danube valley well as a great area of free trade. But free trade was just what the succession states would not dream of granting. Their aim was to secure the maximum of autarky.[1] Politico-economic ambitions here involved a substantial reduction of wealth all round. It is often remarked, for example, that if the forty-eight states of the American Union had been allowed to protect their industries against one another by tariffs, the United States would not be to-day the wealthiest country in the world.

Protective tariffs were not the only wealth-reducing activity of the new or enlarged states. Rumania and in a less degree other states of Central Europe were swept by agrarian revolutions. The great estates of the nobility were torn in pieces and divided up in small parcels among an ignorant peasantry, and peasant proprietorship, if socially the most wholesome, is economically the most inefficient system of agriculture under modern conditions. The peasant has neither the money nor the knowledge nor the enterprise to make use of the techniques which modern science has placed at the disposal of agriculture.

On the whole the Paris Conference deserves little blame, and also, of course, little praise, for the course of events in the old Habsburg Empire.

Bulgaria, under the rule of her German princeling, Ferdinand of Coburg, had joined the wrong side in 1915, when it thought the wrong side was going to win. Thus her frontier problems in relation to her neighbours, Rumania, Jugoslavia, and Greece, were all decided against her. In particular she lost to Greece the strip of coast on the Aegean, which she

---

[1] Autarky means economic self-sufficiency. It is often mistakenly spelt 'autarchy', which would mean no more than political independence, self-rule.

c

had secured from Turkey in the Balkan wars of 1912–13.

Turkey had been proclaimed the 'sick man of Europe' by the Tsar Nicholas I before the Crimean War, and indeed Turkey-in-Europe was doomed and had practically disappeared, apart from Constantinople and some territory near it, a year before the war of 1914–18 began. The Treaty of Sèvres lopped off the Turkish Empire its wide-stretching southeastern provinces, Mesopotamia (Irak), Arabia, Syria, and Palestine, and post-war Turkey has never displayed any ambition to recover these Arabic lands. But the Turk in his native highlands of Anatolia remained, even in defeat, a tough proposition, and the attempt to cut slices off Anatolia in the interests of France, Italy, or Greece constituted a challenge which provoked a violent and successful response. It may seem strange that, while Germany long lay prostrate and did not achieve her resurrection till the 'thirties, Turkey, equally overwhelmingly defeated, should have arisen almost at once and shattered the 'Sèvres porcelain'. An explanation is offered by the greatest of living historians, Arnold J. Toynbee, when he writes: 'Primitive organisms do not suffer so badly from shock as more complicated ones. It was no accident that, of all the defeated powers, Turkey was able to fight a war-after-the-war almost immediately. A low organism is incompetent, but you cannot stun it or kill it as easily as a higher one.' In any case it is a vulgar error to measure the potency of powers by their material dimensions. In these same years Britain, which had played a leading part in defeating Germany, was induced to give way before the 'might' of her Irish rebels.

France staked out claims for herself in Cilicia, the south-eastern province of Anatolia, next door to Arab Syria, in which France has long taken a peculiar interest, though that interest is not reciprocated by the Syrian Arabs. The esurient Italians staked a claim farther west along the same coast, and it was partly in order to restrict the ambitions of Italy that the Peace Conference in 1919, long before there was any Treaty of Sèvres, authorized a Greek expedition to occupy Smyrna. Greece was represented at Paris by the brilliant and fascinating Venizelos, who had a long and stormy career both behind him and ahead of him. The war had brought schism to Greece; half of it under Venizelos had supported the Allies, the other half had remained pro-German under King Constantine, now a dethroned exile. Just as France wanted her Rhine frontier, which she did not get, and Poland wanted the Russian provinces, which had belonged to Poland in the eighteenth century, and got them,[1] so Venizelos wanted the western coastlands of Anatolia, where the seaports had a mainly Greek population. Many of them had been famous Greek city-states in the old days of Classical Greece. So Greek troops occupied Smyrna in the spring of 1919, and almost immediately afterwards the Turkish Nationalists, repudiating the submissive Sultan in Constantinople, established a new government at Ankara in the centre of Anatolia. It was the Sultan in Constantinople and not the government of Mustapha Kemal at Ankara who, in the following year, accepted the Treaty of Sèvres, which allotted extensive territories in western Anatolia to Greece.

[1] This subject will be treated in the chapter on Russia.

In the autumn of 1920, when the Greek armies were established on Anatolian soil beyond the frontier of the territory allotted to Greece by the treaty, the young king of Greece, who was a mere puppet of the Venizelist government, was bitten by a monkey and died. A general election followed, in which the Venizelists were defeated, and the exiled Constantine was restored to his throne. This gave an excuse to those great powers which had never liked the Greek clauses of the treaty, though they had accepted them, to withdraw their support. America had already, through the vote of her Senate soon to be endorsed by an overwhelming anti-Wilsonian victory in the presidential election, washed her hands of all responsibility for European post-war problems. Italy had withdrawn from Anatolia. France not only abandoned her claim to Cilicia, but made a treaty with the Ankara government in accordance with which she sold to it munitions for use against the Greeks. In 1921 Constantine's army boldly advanced on Ankara, but was held up after a ten days' battle fifty miles from the capital. For a year Kemal waited while Greece exhausted herself with the maintenance of an army in the middle of a mountainous and hostile country. At last, in August 1922, he pounced. The Greeks were completely defeated, and not only the Greek army but ultimately the whole Greek population, half a million in number, were either killed or driven out of Anatolia.

Such was the tragedy of Greek ambition. There remained another problem which might have involved disastrous consequences for south-eastern Europe in general. Small Allied forces, British, French, and Italian, still occupied both sides of the historic straits, the Bosporus and the Dardanelles, for the Treaty of Sèvres had arranged that these straits and the city of Constantinople should be placed under international control. If the victorious Turks attacked and overwhelmed these small forces and broke through into Europe, Russia would probably have attacked Rumania, and yet another war might have raged throughout the Balkan countries. The French and Italian forces were withdrawn before the oncoming storm. The British remained behind their entrenchments at Chanak, on the east side of the Dardanelles, and Mustapha Kemal, with a wisdom and moderation which always characterized his dealings with the great powers, refrained from attacking them. An armistice was arranged by the British General Harrington, followed by a peace conference at Lausanne under the presidency of the British Foreign Secretary, Lord Curzon. Turkey obtained not only all Anatolia, but full sovereignty over the straits and an enlargement of her European territory to its 1914 dimensions by the cession from Greece of eastern Thrace.

Lloyd George had acted unwisely, and against the advice of his own foreign office, in encouraging the Greeks in the Anatolian adventure, even after the fall of Venizelos, or at any rate in not firmly discouraging them, but Europe owes him a debt of gratitude for not running away, like the French and Italians, from Chanak. These events were immediately followed by his fall. He was the last of the Big Four of Paris to go. Clemenceau had resigned his premiership and suffered defeat in his contest for the presidency in 1920. Wilson's presidency had ended in 1921, but more than a year before that he had been struck down by mortal illness, brought on by overwork and despair. As for Orlando, scarcely any one outside Italy remembered that there had ever been such a person. Italy, at the date of the Chanak crisis, was just about to entrust herself to Mussolini.

As for Turkey she entered on a course of drastic modernization under Mustapha Kemal, who assumed the surname of Ataturk, which means Chief Turk, and is thus a title of the same significance as Duce and Führer (leader), the titles assumed by Mussolini and Hitler. Turks were compelled to adopt European customs, including bowler hats instead of fezzes, the Latin alphabet, and woman suffrage. Turkey, under Kemal's régime, thus sought to secure her political independence of Europe by adopting European techniques, and in pursuing this policy she was in line with other Oriental communities. This combination of defiance and imitation had long been characteristic of Japan, and was imitated successfully, within more modest limitations, by Ibn Saud of Arabia, and unsuccessfully by Amanullah of Afghanistan, who lost his throne because he tried to go too fast. The anti-British movements in India are also characterized by an intricate mixture of defiance and imitation. Gandhi denounces British rule as satanic, but demands a parliamentary system of which India would never have heard, except from European sources.

As for the Treaty of Lausanne it has survived all the treaties dictated by the Peace Conference from Paris. We have already recorded that the unfortunate Greeks in Anatolia were eliminated. The treaty was followed by a wholesale transference of Greeks from eastern Thrace to Greek territory. Such transferences of population are a painful and barbarous expedient, comparable with the exile of Protestants from Catholic countries, and of Catholics from Protestant countries in an age which was as intolerant on the subject of religion as is the present age on the subject of nationality. But it may well be that the sharp surgical operation of exile involves less pain in the long run than the prolonged penalization of minorities in their old homes under alien rule. When once it is over the memory of it becomes a part of the past. Certainly Greece and Turkey have, since the events here related, been on reasonably good terms with each other, which they would not have been if large numbers of Greeks had remained under Turkish, or large number of Turks under Greek, rule.

THE LEAGUE OF NATIONS

If the war of 1914–18 was really to be a 'war to end war' it must clearly be followed by the establishment of some international institution for the settlement of disputes and the mobilization of immediate and overwhelming force against any state which had the temerity to refuse to accept the terms of settlement offered it. From quite early in the war many minds and many pens were busy with the formulation of ideas on this subject.

From the beginning of the war onwards Sir Edward Grey, the British Foreign Secretary down to the end of 1916, impressed upon Colonel House, Wilson's personal representative, his conviction that the war would never have broken out at all if a conference of the Great Powers, such as Grey had proposed and Germany had rejected in the last days of July 1914, had been a recognized and established institution, and that it was absolutely essential to secure the establishment of some permanent machinery of conference after the end of the war. Before President Wilson delivered the speech in which, America being still a neutral (May 1916), he first publicly committed himself to the policy of a World League of Nations; he secured from House a summary of Grey's views, and based his speech upon it. Less than a year later America declared war on Germany, and in January 1918 the establishment of the League was included among the Fourteen Points. Yet only two months later we find Wilson somewhat nervous on the subject. 'The administrative *constitution* of the League,' he wrote to House in March, 'must grow and *not be made*. We must begin with solemn covenants, covering mutual guarantees of political independence and territorial integrity. . . . Any attempt to begin by putting executive authority into the hands of a group of powers would be to sow a harvest of jealously and mistrust which would spring up and choke the whole thing. The United States Senate would never ratify such a treaty.'

In other words, eight months before the armistice Wilson was unwilling to advance any farther than a 'solemn covenant' without any consequential institution; and the reason for his caution is plain. 'The United States Senate . . .'

Shortly after this the British Government appointed a committee to draw up a constitution for the League, and suggested that the President should establish a parallel committee in America, but he refused to do anything of the kind. Only on the very eve of the armistice does he seem to have persuaded himself, in the intoxication of victory, that he could carry the American Senate and people along with him. Once in Europe he constituted himself the champion of a League constitution almost every idea in which came from a British source. He insisted on the establishment of a committee of the Conference to draft what became known as the Covenant, had himself appointed its chairman, and in spite of French opposition and British scepticism, insisted on the inclusion of the Covenant in the Treaty of Versailles. By this one achievement of a career so largely involved in inconsistency and self-deception, and soon to close in darkness and defeat, the President established, after all, his right to the reputation Europe had accorded him. But in his own country the fate of such a League as he had sponsored was exactly what he had forecast before the illusion of omnipotence descended upon him.

A summary of the Covenant or constitution of the League, with some explanatory notes, will be found in Appendix II of this book, and the reader must be asked to study those pages at this point, for what is recorded there will not be repeated here. We will proceed at once to more general considerations.

The League, it is often remarked, did a great deal of useful work. It not only organized more effectively than any previous body of philanthropists the control of international traffic in drugs and prostitutes, but actually prevented what would almost certainly have been a war between Lilliput and Blefuscu. But the ordinary man refuses to be impressed. It is as though he were told that the doctor cured the patient's chilblains and removed his warts, but could not stop him dying of the disease which the doctor had been called in to deal with. The League did not prevent the repetition of another general war of the great powers, and never at any time looked as if it would be able to do so. Why was this?

It is true, of course, that the League got a bad start. America, the most powerful, and on European questions presumably the most impartial, of the great powers, refused to join. Germany and the other ex-enemy states were refused membership for some years. Russia, in the throes of her Bolshevik revolution, was also excluded. At its inception, therefore, the League consisted of the victorious powers, Great Britain and the British Dominions, France, Italy, Japan, and about fifty other states, scattered all over the world. Some of these, like the republics of South and Central America, were wholly unconcerned with the problems of Europe and little fitted to offer opinions on them, and most of the smaller state members in Europe were more likely to need the help of the League than to contribute to its power and prestige. The presence of Lithuania was poor compensation for the absence of Germany, and the presence of Costa Rica poor compensation for the absence of the United States. The League was, also, not helped by the fact that Lloyd George, the most active mediator in European disputes down to the time of his fall in the autumn of 1922, seemed to regard it as an ornamental rather than a useful institution, and preferred to do business either through the Paris Ambassadors' Conference, which was a sort of 'rump' of the Peace Conference, or through specially summoned conferences at Cannes, Genoa or elsewhere—anywhere but Geneva.

But these drawbacks and rebuffs were not the cause of the failure of the League. The cause lay in its constitution, and its constitution was a faithful reflection of the political ideas current at the time. A glance through the summary of its clauses reveals the weak spots. Except on matters of procedure, all decisions of the Council or the Assembly required a unanimous vote, except where otherwise provided in the Covenant (Art. 5). The League was a League of sovereign states. The states retained their sovereignty. Suppose decisions could have been taken by a majority, a two-thirds or a five-sixths majority, would some great power voting in the minority, Great Britain for example, have been willing to place the British fleet at the disposal of an international committee in Geneva? Obviously not. The world was not ready for a super-national government, and an international government controlled by sovereign states is a contradiction in terms. International institutions can exercise a very powerful influence but, as Washington long ago remarked, 'Influence is not government'.

The radical idealists, Bernard Shaw and H. G. Wells, for example, poured scorn upon the League. This was very easy, but it may have been a salutary exercise if it proved to easy-going optimists in Britain—there were very few easy-going optimists on the other side of the Channel!—that, whatever the League might be, it was not a guaranteed cure for war. Wells set to work on his *Outline of History*, which is, among other things, a magnificent political pamphlet designed to prove that 'the United States of the World' is the ultimate destiny of the human race. It is generally believed that an indescribably painful extinction due to the cooling of the sun is the ultimate destiny of the human race. But we have not got there yet; nor had we in 1919 got to 'the United States of the World'.

Some writer of those days, ingeniously re-punctuating a hackneyed couplet of Tennyson, produced the lines:

> Half a league?—Onward
> Into the Valley of Death.

It was a sound forecast. Because we could only swallow half a League in 1919 we re-entered the Valley of Death in 1939. Yet half a loaf is generally supposed to be better than no bread, and no sub-sequent catastrophe should detract from Wilson's achievement in squeezing the last drops of idealism out of the Dead Sea apples of the Paris Conference. His achievement may be compared with that of Gladstone in his last phase. Gladstone's Home Rule Bills were, unlike Wilson's Covenant, rejected by the Assembly to which they were presented. But if they had been accepted they would almost cer-tainly, like the Covenant, have proved inadequate solutions, for, like the Covenant, they were half-measures. Yet no one can doubt that Gladstone's Irish policy provided a substantial step forward towards the termination of the intolerable nuisance and scandal of British rule in Southern Ireland. At some future date it may become apparent that Wilson stands in the same relation to the S.W.O. (Sovereign World Organization) as Gladstone stands to Eire. In that case Wilson will, no doubt, have the larger grandchild to his credit, though he was certainly not the greater man of the two.

So 'the soldiers won the war and the statesmen lost the peace'. True, but the hackneyed summary is misleading in so far as it suggests that winning the peace was as easy as winning the war; for, however terrible the cost and however astonishing the heroism, winning the war was almost easy, as is proved by the fact that nine Englishmen out of ten, from the first day of the war to the last, were unwaveringly confident that the Allies would win it. In all contests of man with man, from war to football and from football to beggar-my-neighbour, one or other side must win. In war victory will go, granted good management, to the side with the greater resources and, such was the stupid offensiveness of German policy in the present century, that side was, in both the great wars, the side opposed to the Germans. But in the struggle for 'the peace' the statesmen were wrestling 'not against flesh and blood but against principalities, against powers, against the rulers of the darkness of this world, against spiritual wickedness in high places';[1] in simpler language, against the weaknesses and the follies and the vices in the hearts and minds of men. In the last analysis it was the peoples themselves who both won the war in 1914–18 and lost the peace in 1919–39; won it by their indomitable courage and endurance and lost it by their blindness. The statesmen were merely their instruments, and they got into trouble with the peoples that gave them authority not when they were most foolish but when they tried to be wiser than public opinion and the popular press permitted. Clemenceau fell because he had refused to try to incorporate in France a

[1] St. Paul to the Ephesians, vi. 12.

large slice of Germany. Wilson fell because he tried to bring America into a League of Nations. When Lloyd George showed signs, in the spring of 1919, of trying to rise above the mire of his party's general election programme, he received a stern warning from 370 members of the House of Commons, a clear majority of the candidates who had found favour with the electorate three months before.

We shall find the same thing at the other end of the story. It was the people of Germany who gave the Nazis the power to make another war, the peoples of Britain, France, and America who were unwilling that their statesmen should take the steps necessary to prevent it. Successful statesmen cannot in the nature of things be very far in advance of their peoples, a fact which Walter Bagehot indicated with the gentle cynicism of which he was a master when he said that the successful statesman must be a man of first-rate abilities and second-rate creed.

II

THE UPHILL ROAD 1920–29

REPARATIONS AND INTER-ALLIED DEBTS

THE treaty, and agreements subsequent to the treaty, had postponed until May 1921 the settlement—the final settlement as it was called with unconscious irony—of Germany's liability for reparations. Preparation for this event involved the Allied governments in a series of conferences which constitute the most intricate and unprofitable chapter in post-war history, a controversy which forced upon public attention the fundamental disharmony between British and French views. From the British standpoint the war was over and done with. Germany had been so completely defeated and so drastically punished that she was, we assumed, no longer to be feared. We had no warrant in history or in common sense for regarding any nation as a permanent or 'natural' enemy. What we wanted, on grounds of commercial policy and humanity alike, was to expedite by every means in our power the return to normal conditions, in Europe as a whole and above all in Germany. We should have liked to cancel every clause in the treaty which hampered and delayed the return of the normal. It was not that we had been converted to the view (surely an absurd view) that a demand for large-scale reparations from Germany was unjust; we had simply become convinced that it was inexpedient. None the less we had been a party to the treaty and were bound to it—bound to France.

For France, which depended so much less than we did on international trade, the war was not over and done with until it had been paid for. The fruits of victory must be gathered to the very last apple on the tree. If they could not be gathered in the form of reparation payments they must be gathered in some other form. A default in reparations might well enable France to secure, somehow or other, things she had failed to secure under the terms of the treaty. France most emphatically did not look forward to a restoration of normal conditions as the term was commonly understood, namely pre-war conditions without the menace of the Kaiser's army. For France the menace of Germany was a trouble more hard to eradicate than the Kaiser and his works; it was inherent in the fact that there were 70,000,000 Germans and only 40,000,000 Frenchmen. Normal conditions would restore to Germany her natural predominance. The war had brought a victory complete beyond all expectation. The whole purpose of French policy was to secure permanency, by every available device, for the preponderance France enjoyed over Germany in the moment of victory. It was obvious to most people outside France that this French purpose could not possibly be fulfilled. That 'permanency' could in any case be only a matter of a few years, more or less, and the longer the worse, if a long view of future prospects were taken. But practical statesmenship does not easily lend itself to long views, especially under conditions of democracy. The plain man is an opportunist and does not ask to see the distant scene, for he strongly suspects that he could not see it even if he tried. One step enough for him.

As for the Germans, they felt no obligation to facilitate the payment of reparations. The whole conduct of the treaty-making had been such as to inhibit in the German mind any tendency there might have been towards reconciliation and co-operation. They would pay no more then they were forced to pay, and they had every reason to think that the Allies would find that the cost and trouble of extracting reparations were scarcely repaid by the result.

At Paris in January 1921 the Allies agreed to demand from Germany payments for forty-two years to a total amount of £11,000,000,000. In March, Dr. Simons, meeting the Allied statesmen in London, bluntly and rudely refused the demand, offering instead about one-tenth of the amount. The French were inflexible and the British supported them. It was decided to occupy, as a penal measure, Dusseldorf and two other large towns on the right bank of the Rhine. Plans were also made for occupying the whole of the Ruhr valley, far the most important industrial district of Germany, and France broadly hinted that, once in occupation of the Ruhr, she would be slow to give it up.

This venture, however, was postponed for a while. A second conference met in London at which both France and Germany agreed to accept a settlement sufficiently plausible to satisfy the claims of dignity on both sides, and in August payments of reparations were actually begun—by means of a loan to Germany provided by financial houses in London! But the payment of reparations involved the sale of marks in exchange for foreign currencies, and the external value of the mark, had very soon fallen fifty per cent.

Thus began the famous 'flight from the mark' which in the course of the next two years reduced the German paper currency to waste paper and rolled the stone of reparations down to the bottom of the hill again, incidentally ruining the German middle classes and preparing the way for the Nazi revolution —though that was still ten years ahead. The present writer confesses that he does not understand monetary problems. Some authorities say that reparations and the ruin of the mark were related as cause and effect. Others say that the two things are separate and that the latter need not, with proper management on the part of the German Government, have followed the former.

In January 1923 Poincaré, a Lorrainer who represented in its intensest form French hatred of the Germans, had succeeded the more internationally minded Briand as Prime Minister of France. He proceeded to occupy the Ruhr valley with French armies, imagining, as it appears, that the German industries would continue to operate and that the occupying French would skim off their profits. Actually, as might have been expected, the Germans in the Ruhr went on strike with the support, moral and financial, of the Government in Berlin. They were prepared to ruin themselves rather than make profits for France. When the strikes began the mark stood at 50,000 to the pound. The British Conservative Government, under Bonar Law and subsequently under Baldwin, stood aloof from the Ruhr venture, and its law officers expressed a professional opinion that the occupation was not justified by the terms of the Treaty of Versailles.

While reparations were descending into the nether

gulf of Central European bankruptcy the cognate problem of inter-Allied debts was beginning to raise its head above the Atlantic horizon.

When America had entered the war in the spring of 1917 she entered it as an almost unamed belligerent. Her services to the common cause in the field of battle could not become effective until 1918. But there was much that she could do, and did, at once, and among these immediate services was the granting of credits which financed Allied purchases in the United States. The upshot was that Britain emerged from the war owing the Government of the United States nearly £1,000,000,000. This was not, of course, the only inter-Allied debt. France and Italy, and the lesser European Allies (excluding Russia, where the Communist Government had repudiated all debts) owed Britain rather more than Britain owed America. France and Italy also owed smaller sums to America. As things stood in 1922 all these debts were unfunded, interest was being added to the capital account and the creditor was theoretically entitled to demand the repayment of the capital at any time.

It is easy to see to-day that all these debts ought to have been cancelled. Nations allied in war should be assumed to be ready to contribute to the common cause the full strength of all their resources. In the war against Germany one ally, France, being exposed to the full shock of invasion, had contributed far more than her share of the common toll of blood. Britain, serving the common cause less exclusively on the field of fire and more in the factory, contributed less than France to the common roll of honour. There was no means by which we could possibly repay France for her surplus contribution of blood; was it then consistent with human decency that we should demand from France a repayment of our surplus contribution of what are called 'the sinews of war'? And as Britain stood to France in this comparison, so, in a much more marked degree, stood America to all the European allies.

Unhappily the cogency of this argument was obscured, in American eyes, by the reparations demand. The European Allies had set themselves to extract the utmost farthing of damages from Germany. Very well. America demanded no reparations from Germany, but if the European Allies proposed to enrich themselves at Germany's expense, why should America forgo her claims on them?

As early as the summer of 1920 the British Government had begun to realize that there was very little money in reparations, and that without reparations our Continental allies could not, or would not, pay their inter-allied debts. Lloyd George, therefore, addressed the American Government in August of that year suggesting an all-round reduction or cancellation of inter-allied debts, but the proposal was bluntly rejected. The next step lay with America, and in 1922 Congress authorized President Harding to negotiate the funding of the American debts on terms which allowed for no reductions whatever. The British replied, in effect, with a statement of policy known as the Balfour Note. It was addressed not to America but to our own debtors and declared that we would demand from them not a penny more than we were compelled to pay to America. In other words: 'We seek no profit here. If America will be generous to us, all the profit shall be passed on to you.' The publication of the Balfour Note, indicating Uncle Shylock across the water as the villain of the piece, greatly irritated the American public, but in the course of 1923 Baldwin, as Chancellor of the Exchequer, fixed up with the American Government a debt settlement which although very onerous (and involving payments spread over sixty-two years!) was less severe than the terms previously laid down by Congress. Very much more generous settlements were made with the Continental debtors both by America and by Great Britain. None the less, America, while refusing reparations from Germany herself, had forced upon the European allies the strongest possible motive for refusing to abandon their claims to them.

There was quite another respect in which American policy exercised an influence difficult to measure but certainly powerful on European history between the two great wars. Down to 1914 emigration to the United States had been practically unobstructed and 15,000,000 Europeans had availed themselves of the privilege between 1900 and 1914. The war caused an almost complete stoppage of such emigrations but after the war it would certainly have been resumed on an even larger scale if American legislation had not drastically restricted it to about 100,000 a year, distributed among the various nationalities on principles with which we need not trouble ourselves here. Thus a distressed Europe was compelled to retain dissatisfied men and women of the rising generation who would otherwise have emigrated and taken their troubles with them. America was, of course, entirely justified from her own point of view in pursuing this policy, which was imitated by the British Dominions, but it bore hardly on Europe. Discontented young men who might otherwise have emigrated provided the material of De Valera's republican gunmen, of Hitler's Brownshirts and of half a dozen other forces of disturbance.

To return to reparations. The French occupation of the Rhur continued through 1923 and on into 1924, but it was economically a failure since the reparations extracted, though substantial, fell short of the cost of the operation, and it was accompanied by political experiments which not only failed but deserved to fail. These latter were the attempts to foster separatist movements in the parts of the Rhineland occupied by French and Belgian forces —for Belgium, unlike Britain, had shared the French experiment. These separatist governments, if they deserve the name, were set up in flagrant opposition to the will of the inhabitants and included among their members convicted criminals and other discredited adventurers. But what really gave pause to French public opinion was that the franc showed signs of going the way of the mark. One of the French quadrennial general elections took place early in 1924 and registered a marked swing to the Left. Poincaré was defeated and gave place to the more liberal Herriot. At about the same time a general election in Germany gave authority to a government which was prepared to call off the Ruhr strikes as a preliminary to a French withdrawal Nor were these the only favourable factors. After the negotiations of the British-American debt settlement, Baldwin had appealed to the American Government to co-operate in an investigation of Germany's capacity to pay reparations. The reply was favourable, and resulted in the appointment of a committee under the chairmanship of the American representative, General Dawes. Taking as its motto the slogan 'Business, not politics' the Dawes Committee produced an entirely new scheme, the essential feature of which was the establishment in Germany of an international Transfer Committee, under an American chairman, to which reparations should be paid in the new German currency. This committee was to fix the amounts that Germany could and should pay at any given time, and be responsible for the transfer of Germany's payments into the currencies of the creditor states. Another essential feature was to be an initial loan to Germany of £40,000,000, to start up the engine as it were.

These were the cards in Ramsay MacDonald's hands, for he had become Prime Minister and Foreign Secretary of the first British Labour Government in January 1924. He summoned yet another London Reparations Conference, at which Germany and her creditors agreed to accept the Dawes Plan, and France and Belgium undertook to evacuate the Ruhr. 'Almost for the first time in five years,' wrote a British commentator at the time, 'it seems reasonable to expect some alleviation of the plagues that have tormented Europe.' MacDonald, who had been a consistent opponent of the war, was entitled to pride himself on the fact that he had negotiated, just ten years after its beginning and nearly six years after its conclusion, the first amicable settlement between the principal belligerents.

Thereafter, for five or six years, the payment of reparations proceeded, if not 'as merrily as marriage bells', at any rate without serious hitch or disturbance, and it is open to those who hold that Germans respond to no argument except force to say that the occupation of the Ruhr had taught them that further prevarication over reparation payments was likely to involve severe penalties. The economic reconciliation at the London Conference of 1924 was followed, as the next section will show, by a political reconciliation in the following year. It was 'the period of recovery', more particularly the recovery of Germany. German undertakings came to be regarded as good fields for investment, especially in America where an unprecedented prosperity was in full swing. Much more money came into Germany by way of short-term loans than went out of her by way of reparations. Most of it was spent on ambitious designs of industrial reconstruction. In the course of a few years Germany equipped herself, by means of loans from American and British investors, with the most up-to-date plant for industrial production to be found anywhere in the world outside the United States. In the next phase Hitler found it ready to his hand and turned it over to his rearmament programme. Some of the money was paid out in reparations to European creditors, who passed it on in payment of inter-allied debts to America. Thus money made a circle from America to Germany, on to France, Belgium, and Britain, and back to America—though what came *from* America was still on loan requiring repayment some day, as

Germany was to discover in due course to her cost, and to America's.

The Dawes Plan had from the first been regarded as a temporary makeshift. It served its purpose well, but in 1929 all the parties concerned sent representatives to another committee with another American chairman which produced a really final plan, called, after the chairman's name, the Young Plan. This occasioned a violent quarrel, but not with Germany; it was a quarrel between the prospective recipients as to the distribution of the proceeds. But they might have saved their energies for some more useful purpose, for the Young Plan proved final in a more abrupt sense than any one expected. A year later came the 'great slump', and terminated reparation payments for ever. But that lies beyond the confines of this chapter.

SECURITY

Reparations was, after all, only a problem of compensation for past wrongs. Much more important was the establishment of the Rule of Right for the future, and it was to secure this that the League of Nations had been set up. The Covenant had been accepted on the urgent pressure of President Wilson and on the assumption that America would fulfil the duties involved in membership of the organization. But America had refused to join. What did the League amount to without America?

The Covenant was an idealistic and yet also a very cautious document. It laid down the principle that any nation which resorted to war without giving time for the League to invoke arbitration, to try and arrange a peaceful settlement, or at least to

publish to the world an impartial statement of the
matter in dispute with proposals for its peaceful
solution, should be regarded as a common enemy.
At this point the Council or the Assembly of the
League could 'recommend' members of the League
to declare war, but it could go no farther, for each
member was a sovereign state in unimpaired control
of its own policy. Even as regards measures short
of war, 'sanctions' as they were called, a majority
voting for sanctions had no right to call on those
who voted against such a policy to implement it.
After all, every member of the League was as free to
resign its membership as a golfer is to resign from
his golf club. The act of resignation did not constitute the resigning state a 'common enemy'. All
this was natural and inevitable, for the authors
of the Covenant had been faced with the task of
combining incompatible principles. The principle of
absolute state sovereignty and the principle which
came to be called 'collective security', and it was
the principle of collective security that had been
sacrificed to its alternative. In these circumstances
some held that the terms of the Covenant went
dangerously far, that they imposed, or at any rate
suggested, obligations which would prove a snare
and a delusion to those who put their trust in them
because, when it came to the point, the obligations
would not in fact be fulfilled. Others held that the
Covenant did not go far enough, that it was full of
gaps (as indeed it was) and that what was needed
was to stop up the gaps and, as some one said, 'put
teeth into the League'. The view predominating in
Britain and still more in the British Dominions was
that the real security for peace was to be found in

the wisdom and moderation of the various states of the world and that the League was primarily an organ of co-operation, not of coercion, to advise and encourage its members in the pursuit of reasonable policies; and that, where the terms of the Covenant went beyond this, they were unwise and would prove inoperative. In 1920 and again in 1923, Canada moved resolutions designed to render inoperative the crucial articles 10 and 16 and though, owing to the rule requiring a unanimous vote, these resolutions had not been adopted, they had been very widely supported. But in France, and in Poland and Czechoslovakia, both allies of France and likely to be endangered by a German revival, the opposite view prevailed, a view supported also by the propaganda of the British League of Nations Union. These wanted a more cogent Covenant, ensuring that in any outbreak of war all members would be under an obligation to participate actively on the side which the League declared to be right.

A scheme to secure this purpose was prepared in 1923 by a committee of the League under the chairmanship of Lord Robert Cecil, known as the Draft Treaty of Mutual Assistance. The object of the treaty was to induce states to limit their armaments by offering, to those which did so on an agreed scale, guarantees against aggression much more complete than anything offered in the covenant. The guarantees thus offered were on a regional basis, in that the obligation to go to war was limited to states in the same continent as that in which the violation of the Covenant occurred. On these grounds the scheme was objectionable to the British Empire, which would find itself saddled with obligations in every continent. It was rejected by the Labour Government of Ramsay MacDonald.

MacDonald was not, however, content with a gesture of mere rejection, and immediately afterwards attended a meeting of the Assembly of the League in company with the French prime minister, Herriot. It was the first time that prime ministers of great powers had attended a League Assembly. Under the impetus given by their speeches the task was undertaken afresh, and the result was the production of the scheme known as the Protocol (i.e. Draft Treaty) for the Pacific Settlement of International Disputes.

The Protocol aimed at 'stopping up the gaps in the Covenant' and in this it certainly succeeded. Its purpose was to abolish aggressive war by creating a system under which every international dispute should be decided by judicial or arbitral means, and all members of the League were to be under an obligation to go to war with any states which refused to accept such judicial or arbitral awards. This was breath-taking radicalism. The only consolation for the cautious was secreted in a clause which declared that the scheme was not to come into operation unless or until success was achieved in the projected Disarmament Conference of 1925 (which did not in fact meet until 1932).

France ratified the Protocol at once, and so did a number of small states of the kind much in need of protection and not likely to be called on to bear an important part in the task of protecting others. In Britain, however, the scheme was condemned not only by the Conservative Government, which had

recently come into office (Baldwin's second government, 1924–9), but also by Lloyd George and by the
New Statesman. A writer in the quarterly *Round
Table* put the British view in a nutshell when he
wrote:

'It has never been any part of British policy to
sign a blank cheque. . . . There is all the difference
in the world between the influence of the British
Empire being thrown into the scale at Geneva
or elsewhere in accordance with the deliberate
views of its own statesmen, and its being
used at the discretion of five arbitrators sitting
at Geneva.'

Harold Butler, writing in 1942, declares that the
rejection of the Protocol by Britain was 'without
doubt the first turning-point at which the League
turned downhill instead of up',[1] and he compares,
very appropriately, Britain's treatment of the
Protocol in 1924 with America's rejection of the
League four years earlier. But he refrains from
blaming us, and in fact he acknowledges that many
states which acclaimed the Protocol as offering
security for themselves would not have met its
demands if they had been called on to give security
to others. It is in fact only the difference between
the refusal to sign a blank cheque and the refusal to
honour the same cheque at some date subsequent to
its signature. Europe might, with greater wisdom,
have avoided a second great war in the first half of
the twentieth century; it could not have insured
itself against such a war by a document like the

[1] H. Butler, *The Lost Peace*, p. 34.

Protocol, for its peoples had not reached the supernational stage of political development which the Protocol assumed.

From the French point of view the problem of security had become all the more urgent, because January 1925 was the scheduled date under the Treaty of Versailles for the evacuation by Allied troops of one of the three areas into which the Rhineland was divided. January passed without evacuation on the ground that Germany had not yet fulfilled all the Allied demands in the matter of her disarmament, but a policy of postponing evacuation indefinitely on this account or of enforcing by Allied intervention the full rigour of the law in the matter of disarmament would have inevitably kindled to fever-heat again the passions of Franco-German animosity, recently allayed by the acceptance of the Dawes Plan. None of the governments concerned could face this prospect. Instead, the German foreign minister, Stresemann, made proposals in February, which were to provide not only the solution of the immediate Rhineland problem but also an alternative to the Protocol, and gave France, at any rate, a partial satisfaction. These proposals enabled Austen Chamberlain, the British foreign minister, after rejecting the Protocol, to point forward to what subsequently became the Locarno treaties.

The German proposal was that France, Germany, Belgium, and Great Britain should recognize the permanence of the present western frontier of Germany. Briand, the French foreign minister, at once raised the point that France could not disinterest herself in the security of her allies on

Germany's eastern frontier, Poland and Czecho-slovakia. Indeed, the suggested guarantee in the west immediately lowered the political barometer in the east, Poland in particular resenting the suggestion that her own German frontier was less axiomatic than that of France. The implication was, none the less, in accord with the facts as understood in Britain. Alsace and Lorraine were regarded as French by right, whereas the Polish corridor, the separation of Danzig from Germany and the partition of Upper Silesia were hazardous experiments which might, or might not, stand the test of time. We were prepared to guarantee the former, but not the latter.

The conference which met at Locarno in October 1925 had therefore to deal with two frontiers in separate treaties: France, Germany, Belgium, Poland, and Czechoslovakia, the states with the frontiers affected, undertook in no case to go to war with one another, but to invoke arbitration in its place, and abide by its results. Great Britain and Italy guaranteed that this procedure should be observed as regarded the western frontier; France similarly guaranteed the eastern settlement.

The Locarno conference was made the occasion of a variety of festivities expressive of the inauguration of a new era of peace, and its proceedings were followed in England and elsewhere with enthusiasm. It marked, in the words of the *Round Table*, 'the definite termination of the war era'. Less optimistic persons remarked that it involved Britain in a very hazardous commitment. True, we refused to guarantee an eastern frontier in which we did not believe, but could east and west be kept apart? The war of 1914–18 had not originated in a western quarrel, but it had none the less begun with an invasion of France. Suppose a war arose between Germany and Poland on an issue on which British sympathies were predominantly with Germany, and French sympathies with Poland, and suppose that Germany, to secure herself against French attack, violated the French frontier, or even only moved her troops into the demilitarized Rhineland—where would our duty lie under the Locarno treaties? Such speculation may seem perverse to the reader who recalls 1939, but in 1925 there had been no Nazi revolution, and Poland had already defied the western powers by extending her eastern frontier at the expense of Russia far beyond the so-called Curzon line, which had been laid down by the peace conference as her proper eastern limit. At any rate we now did what we had always refused to do before 1914, except in the special case of Belgium; we pledged ourselves in advance to take part in any prospective Franco-German war, on one side or the other.

The immediate item on the Locarno programme was, however, the admission of Germany as a member of the League, and as a permanent member of its Council. About admission to the League there could be no question, but over Germany's admission to a permanent seat on the Council, which implied her recognition as an equal of Great Britain, France, Italy, and Japan, and as superior to all other members, unseemly jealousies arose. Poland, backed by France, claimed a permanent seat also; so did Spain and Brazil. Germany's admission had to be postponed, while new rules for admission to the Council were considered, rules which 'saved the face' of Poland and Spain without actually allotting them permanent seats. Brazil withdrew from the League, which, in any case, could exercise little influence of the affairs of the New World without giving offence to America. None the less, Germany was admitted in 1926, and the speech made on this occasion by Briand should stand on record as evidence of hopes which were not fulfilled.

'Those which indulge in irony and detraction at the expense of the League of Nations', he said, 'and proclaim that it is doomed to perish, what will they think now? . . . Peace for Germany and for France. That means that we have done with the long series of terrible and bloody conflicts which have stained the pages of history. . . . Henceforth our road is to be one of peace and progress. We shall win real greatness for our countries if we persuade them to sacrifice certain of their desires in the service of world peace. The sacrifice will not diminish, it will increase their prestige.'

It is said that professional reporters wept tears of emotion during the delivery of this speech, yet Briand knew very well, even if the reporters did not, that there was an element of make-believe about the whole transaction. The covenant laid down that any state admitted to the League must be proved to have fulfilled its existing international obligations. Germany had notoriously not fulfilled its disarmament obligations under the Treaty of Versailles, and the body entrusted with the supervision of Germany's disarmament, the Inter-Allied Disarmament Control Commission, had prepared a lengthy report specifying in detail the extent of Germany's evasion of her

D

obligations. This report was simply ignored, and remained unpublished. The 'Locarno spirit' must at all cost be preserved even if its preservation required a dose of what later came to be called wishful thinking. Perhaps all would be for the best. Anyhow the thankless labours of the Inter-Allied Disarmament Control Commission were now to be brought to an end. The armaments of a member of the Council of the League could not be subjected the insult of continuous foreign supervision.

Once again we have entered on the 'period of recovery'. For the next few years (1926–9) Britain, France, and Germany, were held together in a reasonable amity by their three foreign ministers. Yet none of the three statesmen on whom this co-operation depended, was entirely trusted in his own country. Austen Chamberlain was often said to be too ready to follow the lead of France. As for Briand, many hard-headed Frenchmen regarded him as a sentimental optimist, building an imaginary security for France on the supposed goodwill of an imaginary Germany. As for Stresemann, what were the secret thoughts of that stout, bald-headed Teuton, outwardly so frank and friendly? In his own country he was widely denounced for his meekness in kissing hands with the authors of the unforgivable *Diktat* of Versailles; but was he perhaps merely biding his time and fooling France with peace-talk until Germany should be ready for revenge? There are passages in Stresemann's papers, published after his death, which suggest that this was so.

One of the signs that the international barometer was not really rising but only remaining steady at a dangerously low level was the failure in disarmament.

After Locarno the Council of the League appointed a body called the Preparatory Commission for the Disarmament Conference, which laboured year after year and produced just nothing on which the principal parties concerned could agree. A little progress, but not much, had been made over naval disarmament. At the Washington Conference of 1921 the five leading naval powers, Great Britain, America, Japan, France, and Italy had accepted a graduated scale of limitation in battleships. Agreement here was easy, for no government felt any great ambition to launch a large fleet of these marine monsters. In 1930, after several failures, Great Britain, America, and Japan accepted limitations to their tonnage in cruisers, destroyers, and submarines, but the two Continental powers, France, and Italy, failed to agree, not with the 'big three', but with each other.

One of the curious events of these years was the so-called Kellogg Pact for the outlawry of war. This was an American project, Kellogg being the American Secretary of State in 1928. The pact was a simple treaty in three clauses, open to the signature of every state in the world. Those who signed it undertook to refrain from war in all circumstances. This seemed very sweeping until the question was raised whether states signing the pact were entitled to fight 'in self-defence'. Kellogg replied that nothing could destroy a nation's right to fight in self-defence, and that each nation must judge for itself when self-defence was required. It is notorious that governments going to war, even Hitler when attacking Poland, assert and believe or pretend to believe that they are fighting in self-defence. Thus the Kellogg Pact may be regarded as entirely meaningless, and it was perhaps for this reason that no country made any difficulty about signing it. The League of Nations was a serious attempt to tackle the problem of the abolition of war: the Kellogg Pact hardly deserves to be so regarded.

SAMPLES OF VIOLENCE

The two previous sections of this chapter have been devoted almost entirely to the history of the relations of defeated Germany with her victorious neighbours and have carried the story, first on the economic and afterwards on the political side, down to a date roughly half-way from the end of the first war to the beginning of the second. The German problem is obviously so very much the most important problem to be considered in this book that no apology need be offered for the large share of the available space accorded to it. None the less, to complete the picture so far given, it seems necessary to frame it by giving some idea of what sort of things were going on outside the Anglo-Franco-German area, in southern and eastern Europe, for example. We have no space for a connected narrative, but must content ourselves with a small assortment of outstanding incidents.

When the first great war began Italy was officially the ally of Germany and Austria, though a proviso had been added to the Triple Alliance exempting Italy from any obligation to join her allies in a war against Britain; for the long Italian coastline would be at the mercy of the British fleet. Availing herself of this proviso Italy remained neutral, and put herself up to auction. Germany and Austria were not prepared to buy her services, because the price demanded was, in the main, Austrian territory; so Italy was knocked down to the highest bidder by the Secret Treaty of London, 1915, and the price was a high one. In the event of an allied victory Italy was to have not only Trieste (which she got) and the Trentino and the southern Tyrol up to the Brenner Pass, with a population of a quarter of a million Germans (which she got), but many other things besides—the Dalmatian coast, Albania, the group of Greek islands called the Dodecanese, which she had already occupied during her war with Turkey in 1911, a slice of southern Anatolia, and, in the event of Great Britain or France increasing their colonial possessions in Africa at the expense of Germany, an 'equitable compensation' in that continent, which to Italian minds was another way of saying Abyssinia. At the Peace Conference President Wilson not only declared that he would not regard this treaty as binding on himself but that it had been superseded and rendered invalid by Italy's acceptance of the Fourteen Points. Indeed he went farther than this; in the strength of his singular delusion that he alone of the statesmen at the Peace Conference represented 'the sentiments of mankind', he issued an appeal to the Italian people over the heads of their own representative statesmen. This annoyed Italians so much that the people of Genoa, having no American emblem at hand on which to express their feelings, proceeded to throw stones at the statue of their famous fellow-citizen, Christopher Columbus.[1]

Let us take these Italian demands and consider

[1] I hope this story, current at the time, is true. If it is not it ought to be.

their subsequent history. Abyssinia must be left until a later chapter. Italy abandoned her slice of Anatolia when Mustapha Kemal began to look alarming, but held on to the Dodecanese because there was nothing very alarming about Greece. She occupied Albania for two years, and was then turned out by the Albanians. As for Dalmatia, that was now claimed, on grounds of self-determination by Jugoslavia, which had replaced the Habsburg monarchy in that part of the world, and Italy gave up her demand for it. But there was a port named Fiume, also inhabited by Jugoslavs, between Dalmatia and Trieste, which Italy wanted much more than Dalmatia, but had by some oversight forgotten to include in the Treaty of London. The Paris Conference refused it to Italy, but it was lawlessly occupied in September 1919 by a private venture expedition under the Italian poet, D'Annunzio, and after many negotiations remained in Italian hands throughout the inter-war period.

In August 1923 an Italian general was murdered on Greek soil, and Italy dispatched to Greece an ultimatum similar in tone to the notorious Austrian ultimatum to Serbia in July 1914, after the murder of the Archduke, which precipitated the first great war. Greece made a reply as submissive as that of Serbia on the earlier occasion, and the Italian Government, which was now Mussolini, retorted by occupying Corfu. Greece appealed to the League, which ordered Greece to buy the Italians out of Corfu by the payment of a substantial fine.

In 1925 a quarrel arose between Greece and Bulgaria of which it may be said, without going into tiresome details, that both sides were to blame.

Greece invaded Bulgaria. The League intervened, stopped the war and imposed a settlement. This is the occasion which we referred to somewhat irreverently on an earlier page as the stopping of a war between Lilliput and Blefusen. It was hailed by the world in general as a triumph of the League, but a British historian of modern Greece writes:

> 'It was felt at the time in Athens that Greece had been sacrificed a second time to save the prestige of the League, which turned the left cheek to great powers but extorted the uttermost farthing from small states.'[1]

Poland was annoyed by the establishment of an independent Lithuania since, for some centuries before the extinction of the old Polish Kingdom in 1795, Lithuania had been united with the Polish state. Vilna was recognized by the Paris Conference as the capital of Lithuania, but for some time it passed backwards and forwards between the Lithuanians and the Russian Bolsheviks in a most bewildering manner. Finally it was seized by a Polish general in October 1920. The League protested but Poland stood firm. Two and a half years later Polish violence was rewarded, and the Conference of Ambassadors in Paris, which had already been mentioned as a kind of rival authority to the League in the early post-war years, declared Vilna to be part of Poland.

Under the twenty-second article of the Covenant the colonies taken from Germany were not to be annexed outright by the victors, but entrusted to them under mandates, and the states entrusted with the government of these territories were to be

[1] W. R. Miller, *Greece*, p. 94.

responsible for their administration to a committee of the League, to which they had to submit annual reports. This implied a recognition of the principle that the backward and primitive peoples of the world ought not to be treated as the property of various imperialist powers and exploited for the benefit of their masters, but governed on the principle that (in the words of the Covenant) 'the well-being and development of such peoples form a sacred trust of civilization'. Similarly, certain parts of what had been the Asiatic Empire of Turkey were entrusted to great powers under mandates, though these mandates were of a different character and intended to be temporary. Iraq and Palestine were allocated to Great Britain, and the coastal region of Syria to France. The mandatory system proved unacceptable to the Iraqi Arabs, and an Anglo-Iraqi treaty was substituted for it, in accordance with which British officials assisted the government of King Feisal, the former comrade-in-arms of Colonel Lawrence, in a manner which gave general satisfaction. In Palestine the British Government shouldered the impossible task of providing a 'national home for the Jews' in such a manner as to satisfy the Jewish hopes raised by the Balfour Declaration of 1917, without at the same time breaking the pledge given to the native Arabs in the same Declaration that 'nothing shall be done which may prejudice the civil and religious rights of the non-Jewish population'.

The difficulties of the British in Palestine were due to the impossible nature of the task which the mandate and the Balfour Declaration imposed upon them, whereas the difficulties of the French in Syria were due to the fact that they had no intention of carrying out the mandate on the terms laid down. Their aims and their methods from the first were those of a camouflaged annexation. There was a further difficulty as to the area within which the mandatory power was to exercise authority. A Franco-British agreement made during the war, the Sykes-Picot agreement, limited French control to a coastal strip, and envisaged one or more independent Arab states in the hinterland. Indeed, at the time of the armistice the Emir Feisal, already mentioned as subsequently King of Iraq, was established in Damascus with the approval of the British Government. When British troops withdrew from Syria the French proceeded to pick a quarrel with Feisal and drove him out. In fact the French aim was to make Syria a province of her Mediterranean Empire, and though in the long run she failed, the failure was due to the opposition of certain sections of the local inhabitants and not to any control enforced upon her by the League, whose mandate she was ignoring.

There is a certain monotony about the catalogue of incidents just recorded, for they all illustrate the same fact: that in a world constituted as was the world of the 1920's, quite a small amount of force, exerted by a single state which knew what it wanted and was determined to get it, could quite successfully defy the vast forces theoretically at the disposal of an international authority dedicated to ideals in which most of its members did not really believe.

III

NATIONAL HISTORIES

INTRODUCTION

THERE are two ways of dealing with subjects like that of this book. One way is to concentrate on the history of international relations, omitting the domestic histories of each state or, where they cannot be entirely omitted, introducing them parenthetically as it were, as opportunity offers. The previous chapter gave a history of certain international relations on these lines, but it has obviously left many gaps, for some domestic events are quite as important as any international events in their contribution to the general history of the period between the two wars. The other way is to take each nation state in turn and offer a picture of its national experience, showing, for example, both the domestic events and the foreign policy of France or Germany as the experience of France or Germany. To carry this method to its logical conclusion would of course involve a great deal of duplication, for a Franco-German quarrel is both part of the history of France and part of the history of Germany.

In the present chapter the second of these courses will be pursued. The principal nation states of the western world will be taken in turn and their histories reviewed, in so far as their histories are important to an understanding of the problem of this book. The order in which they have been arranged is not fortuitous. Russia is placed first because the most important Russian event, the Bolshevik or Communist revolution, occurred at the very beginning, or rather just before the beginning, of our period. Italy comes next, because her great domestic event, the Fascist revolution, marks the beginning of the general drift from democracy to anti-communist dictatorship. Germany naturally follows, and after Germany a collection of the smaller states on Germany's eastern frontier. Finally, at increasing distances from Germany on the western side, France, Great Britain, and the United States. Each of these historical sketches will begin with the beginning of our period, but they will not be carried down to the end of it; each will be broken off at what seems a convenient point in relation to the arrangement of the rest of the book.

RUSSIA

The Russian revolution resembles the French revolution and also, with rather wider differences of detail, the English Puritan revolution in that all three showed rapid and violent transitions from traditional monarchy to parliamentarism, from parliamentarism to dogmatic idealism, and from dogmatic idealism to a dictatorship which might still pay lip-service to idealism, but was in essentials a dictatorship of efficiency and common sense. Charles I, the Long Parliament, the 'Saints', Cromwell; Louis XVI, the National Assembly, the Jacobins, Napoleon; the Tsar, the Kerensky Liberals, the revolutionary communists, Stalin. Space forbids more than a short-hand indication of an attractive set of parallels.

The outbreak of the Russian revolution in March

1917 was not due to communism, but to hatred of the war. The Russian armies and, so far as they played an active part, the Russian people, could not stand it any longer. There were bread riots in Petrograd (erstwhile Petersburg and soon to be renamed Leningrad), and the soldiers joined the rioters. The Tsar abdicated, and a parliamentary government was formed in which an eloquent lawyer named Kerensky soon took the lead. This government professed itself anxious to carry on the war and resume the offensive against Germany, but the longing for peace at any price, which had taken hold of the Russian armies and people, was too strong. The Russian offensive of 1917 produced only mutiny, defeat, and wholesale desertion.

Meanwhile the Germans had taken an extraordinary step. There were living in Switzerland certain Russian communist exiles, among them Lenin. These men the German Government offered to transport across Germany to Russia, much as though—supposing the threatened fantasy of bacteriological warfare were ever realized—one might transport a consignment of cholera bugs into enemy territory. The offer was accepted and, once arrived in Russia, these 'bugs' (from the German point of view) got to work with diligence and skill to make a second revolution which would overthrow Kerensky and the liberals and make peace immediately. They succeeded, and in November Trotsky, the military organizer of the party, secured possession of Petrograd.ᶜ In December the Russian communists made peace with Germany at Brest-Litovsk, ceding to Germany, to dispose of according to her pleasure 'and the will of the inhabitants', not only Finland,

Poland, and the Baltic provinces between them, but also the whole of southern Russia, the Ukraine. The communists were not interested in national frontiers. They thought that they were inaugurating not a Russian but a world revolution, and they held that, the more German imperialism overreached itself, the more likely it was to succumb to Communism in the long run. It is, of course, also true that Russia was at Germany's mercy, and that the communists had to make the best of a bad job.

It was the desertion of the common Allied cause by the communists which enabled Germany to make those alarmingly successful attacks on the western front in the spring of 1918, which preceded her own collapse in the autumn of the same year.

The statesmen of the victorious Allies assembled at the Peace Conference in 1919 did not know what to do about Russia. President Wilson had devoted the longest of his Fourteen Points to the subject,[1] but it was of no avail. Offers to arrange a meeting with the communist leaders were refused, and that was not surprising, since the western powers were in fact at war with the communist government. From the standpoint of the Allies fighting Germany in 1918 the communists had been 'collaborationists', 'quislings' (to use the jargon of the next war), and we were justified in supporting any 'underground movement' in Russia which aimed at their over-throw. Afterwards when the German war suddenly ended, we could not in honour desert the 'White' Russian forces we had hitherto sustained, and we had vast quantities of surplus munitions left over from our own war which might as well go to them as

[1] See Appendix I.

to the scrap-heap. But the upshot of the Russian civil war of 1919 was that the Soviet Government (as it was beginning to call itself) in Moscow triumphed over all its 'White' rivals and reconquered the Ukraine, which had been occupied by royalist forces after the withdrawal of the Germans.

Having defeated its Russian enemies the Communist Government was confronted with the problem of Poland. The old kingdom of Poland had included extensive territories in which, though the land-owning class was largely Polish, the bulk of the population was Russian. The new Poland, under its leader, Pilsudski, was determined to annex these territories in spite of the fact that the Peace Conference had drawn an eastern frontier for Poland, called the Curzon line after Lord Curzon, British foreign secretary at the time, which roughly corresponded with the limit of the territory within which Poles constituted a majority of the population. Poland invaded Russia and was defeated. Russia in turn invaded Poland and pressed right up the Vistula opposite Warsaw. Western Europe was seriously alarmed. Nothing but a demoralized Polish army stood between the forces of revolutionary communism and prostrate Germany, where a feeble republican government was struggling with every kind of difficulty. France sent Weygand, the right-hand man of Foch, to advise the Poles, and there occurred in August 1920 'the miracle of the Vistula'. The communists were defeated and rolled back into Russia. Poland secured, unfortunately for herself in the long run, all the eastern provinces beyond the proper limits of Poland which it was her ambition to secure.

The battle of the Vistula, though fought with armies that would have counted for next to nothing on the western front of 1914–18, has been regarded as a decisive battle of history, comparable with the battle of the Marne. The battle of the Marne secured that western Europe should not be placed under the heel of Prussian militarism; the battle of the Vistula secured that central Europe should not be delivered over to Russian communism. Putting it another way, one may say that the events of 1918–20 had provided answers to two questions: first, would communism succeed in establishing itself in Russia? Secondly, would it succeed in establishing itself in other parts of Europe? By the end of 1920 both these questions had been fairly definitely answered, the first in the affirmative, and the second in the negative. In Russia it had come to stay: elsewhere it had failed. Communist governments in Hungary and Bavaria had been easily suppressed after a very brief existence. However, before proceeding farther it may be well to attempt a short answer to the question, what is communism?

Communism is a theory of society and a programme of revolutionary action elaborated by a German Jew named Karl Marx, resident for the most part in London during the middle years of the reign of Queen Victoria, and embodied by him in an enormous book called *Capital*. Not only did he write his book, but he organized an International Working Men's Association, commonly called 'The International', for the promotion of his ideas. Partly perhaps because he was a Jew, Marx regarded national divisions and rivalries as unreal and likely to disappear at no very distant date. In his view the only

real division of society was between the 'haves' and
the 'have nots', or, as he called them, the *bourgeoisie*,
or middle class who had practically absorbed and
superseded the nobility in all progressive countries,
and the *proletariat*, a word of Latin derivation,
meaning those who own nothing but their own
bodies and their children. His slogan, issued as early
as 1847, was 'Workers of the world, unite; you have
nothing to lose but your chains'.

History had hitherto shown that national divisions, however absurd and deplorable they might be,
counted for more than class divisions. Marx's first
International was destroyed by the Franco-German
war of 1870. The second was destroyed by the war
of 1914–18. The Russian Communist Government
established, as a propaganda department of itself, a
third International, known as the Comintern.

The doctrines of communism were based on a study
of the evil effects of the industrial revolution on the
security of the working classes, and Marx would have
been surprised if he could have known that the first
country to give a trial to his system would be a vast
backward country in which the bulk of the population were peasants working on the land. But
extremists owe their opportunities to the collapse of
organized government. Government collapsed in
Russia, and the tiny communist group succeeded in
stepping into the breach, partly because they offered
the peasant ownership of his land (which is not
communism at all), and still more because they
offered immediate peace.

The leading idea of communism is class war. The
bourgeoisie, who are represented as parasites living
on the profits of other people's labour, must be

'liquidated', or destroyed; and in Russia they were destroyed to the accompaniment of widespread atrocities, which were denounced by those in other countries who hated and dreaded communism and minimized by 'left-wing' parties which, without being communist, inclined towards socialistic solutions. A 'dictatorship of the proletariat' was to be set up, which in due course would organize a perfectly communistic society. When it had done so the dictatorship was to disappear. But a perfectly communistic society has never existed outside the covers of a book. For practical purposes communism means a dictatorship in the supposed interests of the working classes. The Russian statesmen accepted the works of Marx as their holy scriptures, but these holy scriptures, like other holy scriptures, were full of difficult passages which could not be literally applied; and those who championed the scriptures most loudly had often a somewhat vague idea of their contents. At any rate they were prepared to depart from them when a too literal acceptance of their teachings produced disastrous results. For example, the land had been given to the peasants, but in accordance with communistic doctrine the produce of the land belonged to the state, and the workers on the land were only entitled to as much of the produce as was necessary for their own sustenance. The result was that the peasant tended to grow only as much produce as he required for himself. Thereupon a great many peasants were 'liquidated', but none the less Russia suffered in 1920 and 1921 the severest famine that had afflicted any part of Europe since the Irish potato famine of 1845. In response Lenin adopted what was called the 'new economic policy', which was in fact an abandonment of communism and a return to private enterprise on a large part of the field of production.

When it became obvious that communist revolutions in central and western Europe could not be expected in the immediate future the Russian Government set itself to re-establish amicable relations with its neighbours, to reopen the courses of trade and to secure recognition as a legitimate government. True to their policy of letting bygones be bygones and endeavouring to set the wheels of what Americans call 'normalcy' in motion, the British Government were the first to negotiate a trade agreement with Russia in March 1921, and in January of the following year Lloyd George invited Russian delegates to an international conference at Cannes, with a view to a political settlement. But negotiations broke down over the question of the repudiated Russian debts, and the only tangible result was that Russia concluded a treaty not with any of the Allies but with Germany. This Treaty of Rapallo was so much more important to Germany than to Russia that it will be best to consider it elsewhere

It was undoubtedly difficult to deal with the Russian Government, because it spoke with two voices. Chicherin, the foreign minister, conducted negotiations after the traditional pattern as the representative of a national state making a friendly business deal with one of its neighbours, while at the same time the Jew, Zinoviev, who presided over the Third International or propaganda department, was inciting foreign communist parties to overthrow the very governments with which Chicherin was doing business. A striking example of these tactics was furnished by Anglo-Russian relations in 1924. The British Labour Government had just, for the first time, accorded full recognition *de jure* to the Soviet Government, and intended to assist the restoration of Russian credit by means of a loan guaranteed by the British Government. It became apparent that this loan would not be acceptable to the House of Commons, and MacDonald dissolved parliament in the hope of securing a pro-Russian majority. This was the moment selected by Zinoviev for addressing a letter to the British communist party, a minute organization of no importance, urging on them the duty of violently overthrowing the British constitution. The letter came into the possession of the Foreign Office, and was published five days before the election—which resulted in a substantial Conservative majority.[1]

Zinoviev's propaganda was, indeed, extremely unsuccessful. It failed to make anything out of what might have been thought to be two excellent opportunities. The French occupation of the Ruhr (1923), and the British coal crisis and general strike (1926). The British Trades Union Congress refused to accept the substantial Russian funds offered them for the prolongation of the general strike, and though the miners' union accepted Russian support during the prolonged coal strike which continued after the collapse of the general strike, this fact in no way

[1] This result was in any case probable, and the influence of the letter on the election has been commonly exaggerated. It has sometimes been asserted that the Zinoviev letter was a forgery, but there is no good reason for thinking so. Zinoviev often sent out letters of this kind.

improved the prospects of British communism. In the following year the continuance of Russian communist propaganda persuaded the Home Secretary to authorize a police raid on the premises of the Soviet commercial organization in London, known as Arcos. Ltd. Various compromising documents were found, on the strength of which the British Government cancelled the trade agreement of 1921.

In January 1924 Lenin had died after a long illness—a mysterious, bloodstained but impressive figure—and after his death the conflict between what we have called the 'two voices' became a life-and-death struggle between rival factions for the control of the Russian Government; on the one side the nationalists led by Stalin, and on the other the international revolutionists, many of them Jews, led by Trotsky. The nationalists won, and in 1927 Trotsky, Zinoviev and others were expelled from the government. Some, like Trotsky, fled the country, never to return; others, like Zinoviev, were arrested, convicted of treason, and executed. These trials had nothing to do with 'justice', as the term is understood in England; they were comparable rather with the procedures by which one gang of Jacobins got rid of another during the French Reign of Terror.

As soon as he was in control of the government Stalin imposed on the country his industrial Five Year Plan (1927–32), followed on its completion by 'the mixture as before'. Visitors to Russia at the end of the period of the first Plan remarked that the average Russian seemed to be as poor as ever, but Stalin's object was not to make the average Russian comfortable; he was engaged in forcibly industrializing Russia. Just as the Germans a few years later were compelled by Nazi policy to prefer guns to butter, so Stalin's Russians were compelled to prefer imported machinery to home-grown food, for the food had to be exported to pay for the machinery. The published statistics of increased industrial production were so astonishing that most people abroad refused to believe them, but the performance of the Russian war industries in and after 1941 has since proved that the Five Year Plans achieved their object.

Of course there were failures and breakdowns here and there, and when these occurred the Russian authorities set themselves to prove that the foreign manufacturers of imported machinery or the foreign engineers imported to direct its operations were the villains of the piece. In 1933, in consequence of the breakdown of an important power station, the Russian Government arrested and accused of sabotage certain British engineers employed in Russia by the Metropolitan Vickers Company. The Russian trial of the engineers was similar in character to the Nazi Reichstag trial, which took place in the same year. The Nazis wished to 'prove' that the Reichstag had been burnt down by foreign communists, and the Russians to 'prove' that the power station had been put out of action by foreign capitalists; and of course neither government had any difficulty in 'proving' what they wanted. The engineers were, however, released after brief terms of imprisonment.

Thus Russia's relations with Great Britain were not agreeable. French feeling was still more hostile, partly on account of the large number of White *émigrés* in France, partly on account of the large number of French investors in the repudiated Russian loans, and partly because in France, unlike Britain, the local communist party was sufficiently large to be alarming. Russo-German relations during the years before the Nazi revolution were generally friendly. Towards her neighbours on her western frontier Russian policy was entirely unaggressive, for the undeveloped territories already at her disposal, from the frontier of Poland to the frontier of Manchuria, were so vast that she required no more. She had good claims against both Poland and Rumania, but she did not press them. Such states as Latvia and Estonia were absolutely at her mercy, but she seemed contented to accept the Brest-Litovsk frontier which had undone the work of Peter the Great, and pushed her back from the whole Baltic coast except at the top of the Gulf of Finland below Leningrad.

The rise of Hitler, with his declared policy of creating a *Lebensraum* (living-space) for Germany at the expense of Russia, led to a rapid transformation of Russian foreign policy. Hitherto she had denounced the League as an abominable alliance of the forces of world capitalism. Now she was ready to join it, and did so in 1934, being given, without opposition, a permanent seat on the Council. In the following year Russia concluded treaties of mutual assistance in case of attack with France and Czechoslovakia.

ITALY

Italy had entered the first great war from motives entirely different from those actuating Britain, France, and Russia. These others were engaged in defending themselves against Prussian militarism.

Italy was not directly threatened by Germany at all; she entered the war to get what she could at the expense of the moribund Habsburg Empire. She got a good deal but not as much as she had hoped. Moreover, her representatives were treated with scant respect by Clemenceau and to moral lectures by Wilson. She was wounded in her self-esteem, and this was with Italy a very susceptible organ. She was rather like a character in a novel I have read and cannot identify, who 'spent most of his time wondering whether he was or was not a gentleman'. Italy spent a good deal of time wondering whether she was or was not a great power. Officially she had been recognized as such since her union in 1860, but she was well aware that the other great powers were well aware that her claims to the reality of great powerdom were somewhat unsubstantial.

There was also another cause of trouble. Cavour, the principal architect of Italian unity, had combined a diplomacy worthy of Machiavelli with a whole-hearted admiration of British parliamentary institutions. United Italy had been provided with a parliamentary system, and Cavour had died immediately afterwards without being given time to show whether his genius could infuse life into it. For parliamentary government requires much more than the establishment, on paper, of a parliamentary constitution. If it is to work well, there must be an intelligent democracy of voters and a class of persons ready to offer themselves for service in parliament who are not only intelligent but also honest and patriotic. Great Britain has enjoyed the inestimable advantage of having learnt to operate a parliamentary government, first on an aristocratic and afterwards on a middle-class basis, long before she became a democracy. Many of the countries that adopted parliamentary government and democracy simultaneously, either in the nineteenth century or after the first great war, proved themselves quite unfit for this type of constitution, and a parliamentary government where the electorate is ignorant and the elected members adventurers or rogues, is as bad a government as can be imagined. Such was the case in Italy. The system had not worked well even before the war, and the post-war years presented a complex of domestic problems which proved a severe test of even the most experienced and well-established governments. The Italian parliamentary politicians failed completely when confronted with this test. Strikes, riots, street warfare of rival partisan forces were rampant in all the big towns, among them the *fascio di combattimento*, or union of ex-soldiers. A great deal can be said against the régime Mussolini, the leader of the Fascists, established, but this also must be admitted, that the régime he overthrew had proved itself unable to govern.

The best description known to me of the origins of Italian Fascism is to be found in *The Lost Peace*, by Harold Butler, a man who cannot be accused of any sympathy with Fascism as it ultimately worked out:

'Both in Italy and in Germany Fascism began as a revolt of the youth of the lower middle class against the miseries and ruin of the war and its aftermath. They saw no future before them. Their families had usually lost their savings, the professions were overcrowded, opportunities of

economic advancement were too limited to give
them a prospect of marrying and earning a decent
income. When they were offered not only jobs but
an ideal, the moral and material rehabilitation of
their country, many of the best young men felt
that they had found something worth living for,
something more inspiring than mere money-
grabbing, a dazzling chance of unlimited national
service. . . . In both countries the rank and file and
many of the leaders of the totalitarian party were
recruited from the hooligans, the ne'er-do-wells,
and the adventurers, who saw in it the chance of
obtaining money and power which they could not
hope to acquire in a well-ordered society. Neither
in Germany nor in Italy, however, would the
appeal have been so effective if it had not contained the promise that the power of big business
would be curbed by the state, and that the
country should be run for the benefit of the whole
people regardless of the privileges of capital and
labour alike.'[1]

By the autumn of 1922 things had got so bad that
Mussolini decided that his fascists should march on
Rome and impose their will on the government. The
prime minister asked the king to issue a proclamation
establishing martial law. He refused; the prime
minister resigned, and the king sent for Mussolini,
inviting him to take the office of prime minister and
form a government (30 October 1922). It was an
almost bloodless revolution.

At first Mussolini preserved the externals of
parliamentary government, and it was not till

[1] H. Butler, *The Lost Peace*, p. 182–3.

several years later that the parliament was abolished and Mussolini assumed the title of the *Duce*. He also began by allowing freedom of the press, but abolished it in 1923 owing to the venomous attacks of the Liberals. Indeed it is clear that Mussolini was only gradually brought to establish an absolute tyranny such as Lenin and Hitler had intended from the first. By preserving the monarchy and, in 1929, making a treaty with the Pope, he secured the support of the conservative classes. By restoring order and enabling industry to recover he proved that his system could give the 'better times' it promised. He was indeed fortunate in that he seized power at a time when trade all over the world was taking a turn for the better after the first post-war slump. His government also undertook and carried through great public works, such as the draining of the Pontine Marshes, a once fertile district which had lain derelict for two thousand years, since the war of the Roman Republic with Hannibal. To lovers of freedom he had of course nothing to offer.

Something has already been said about the predatory activities of Italy during the first post-war years. France, the only other Mediterranean great power, was Italy's natural rival, and ill-feeling was increased by the fact that France gave a home to many of the Italian Liberals who fled from Mussolini's régime. Moreover, France owned territories which many Italians thought ought to belong to Italy: Tunis, where Italian settlers outnumbered the French, and Corsica, where Italian was the native language. Throughout the 1920's Italy and France competed for the goodwill of the Danubian states. We had already seen that Italy and France failed to agree,

in 1930, on a plan for the limitation of their navies.
Italy claimed naval equality with France. France
claimed a larger navy on the ground that she had
two seas to guard, the Atlantic and the Mediterranean, whereas Italy had only one. If their fleets were
equal Italy would in fact be the superior power in
the Mediterranean. Italy retorted that if France
were granted superiority, she could overawe Italy by
bringing her whole fleet round to the Mediterreanean.
The counter-arguments illustrate the difficulty, indeed the impossibility, of arranging agreed limitations
of armaments until security and mutual trust have
first been achieved. To aim at security by means
of disarmament is to put the cart before the horse.

One of the most oppressive undertakings of the
Fascist government was the enforced Italianization
of the Germans in the newly acquired Tyrolese
province, by the suppression of their schools and
newspapers. The misfortunes of these Germans
evoked much sympathy in England, but Hitler, otherwise so solicitous of the welfare of Germans outside
Germany, never raised a finger on their behalf.

The Nazi revolution in Germany gave a new turn
to Mussolini's policy, as to Stalin's. His first proposal
in 1933, was a Four Power Pact of Italy, Germany,
France, and Great Britain, having 'as its general
purpose, peace, and as its big and almost only detail,
a revision of the treaties', i.e. the peace treaties of
1919. Nothing came of this.

In 1934, when Hitler announced that Germany
was going to rearm, Mussolini joined Great Britain
and France in a conference held on Italian soil at
Stresa, and put his signature to the stern rebuke
issued to Germany on this occasion. There is no

doubt that Mussolini was genuinely alarmed by the resurgence of Germany, which he foresaw would involve the absorption of Austria and the advance of the forces of the Reich right up to the Italian frontier. But he was also at this time very anxious to stand well with France and Britain, for he was already preparing the ground for his great imperial venture, the conquest of Abyssinia.

GERMANY

It has often been remarked that Ludendorff, the Chief of Staff of the German armies of the western front, signalled to his government that all was up, in the autumn of 1918, before in fact the armies under his command had been decisively defeated. If it were the custom of belligerents to behave with the rationality of professional chess players and abandon the game as soon as they perceived that the victory of their opponents was inevitable, no question would arise; but this is notoriously not so. Ludendorff's behaviour was, in so keen a professional soldier, most exceptional. It may be, of course, that he simply lost his nerve, but it is possible that he was looking to the future, and that his object was to preserve for some future occasion as much of the essential framework of the German army as he could. That certainly was the result achieved.[1] In spite of the

---

[1] Ludendorff remarked at the time, according to his Memoirs: 'I want to save my army.' His idea was that it would prove a valuable instrument of blackmail during the peace negotiations, for he seems to have supposed that the Allies would be so simple minded as to leave its armament intact under the terms of the armistice. Foch, however, insisted, against the wishes of President Wilson, that the bulk of the German guns, tanks, and aeroplanes should be surrendered.

disarmament clauses of the Treaty of Versailles, much of the German army, and the traditions of the German army, survived fragmentarily in the 'Free Corps', which played a prominent part in the domestic upheavals of the Republic. The version of the facts afterwards put into currency by the Nazis, that Germany owed her defeat to some unidentifiable 'stab in the back' engineered by the Jews, has no relation whatever to the facts of history.

People talk about the German democratic revolution of November 1918, but there was no revolution at all. The Allied governments had often declared during the war that they would never make peace with 'Prussian militarism', and President Wilson, in his dispatch to the last Chancellor of the Empire during the pre-armistice negotiations, had indicated that he could not treat with the Kaiser. Accordingly, two days before the armistice, the Kaiser was persuaded or forced to abdicate by German soldiers and statesmen of the old régime who thought the country might get better terms if he was out of the way. He fled to Holland, and at the same time all the minor German royalties, kings of Bavaria, Saxony and the like, who had continued to discharge more or less ornamental functions within the framework of Bismarck's federated Empire, abdicated and disappeared. In the words of a German writer, they just 'went out, like a lamp that had come to the end of its oil'. A German Republic was proclaimed; but Germany did not become a republic through any passion for republicanism such as had animated large sections of the American and French peoples at the end of the eighteenth century. Germany became a republic because Germans of all classes thought that if their country assumed the guise of a republic it would be more likely to enlist the sympathies of President Wilson.

The old ruling class slipped away in face of the disaster which their militarism had provoked, and left the unenviable task of governing Germany to the Majority Socialists. These were the men who, though opposing the Kaiser's policy in the Reichstag before the war, had swallowed their convictions and supported the war effort from August 1914 onwards. By 1918 they were not really socialists at all, but much more like Liberal-Labour men. Like all Continental liberals throughout the nineteenth century they desired a parliamentary form of government, and as Labour men—many of them were trade union leaders—they desired to improve the position of the wage-earning classes, who had been ruthlessly exploited by the big business interests during the war. One of them, Ebert, a saddler by origin, became the first president of the republic, and held the post till his death in 1925. Another, Scheidemann, became the first of its many chancellors, i.e. prime ministers, for ministries were to change almost as frequently and as meaninglessly in the German republic as in the French one. A third, Noske, became minister of police. These men and their colleagues and successors have been as completely and deservedly forgotten as the last prime ministers of parliamentary Italy. Never was a feebler lot of men called upon to govern a potentially great nation. Circumstances had pushed them into the position of leaders, but there was no leadership in them.

There were, of course, also real social revolutionists

in Germany, the Minority Socialists under Lieb-knecht. They had opposed the war from the start, and many of them had spent most of its duration in prison, but were now released. They were called Spartacists, taking the name from a series of com-munist pamphlets, published over the signature 'Spartacus', the original Spartacus having been the leader of an insurrection of slaves in Ancient Rome. The first serious problem of the new government was to deal with these Spartacists, who seized Berlin in January 1919. For strong men crises are oppor-tunities. The Spartacus rising provided the govern-ment with an excellent opportunity for creating a republican volunteer militia under republican leaders, but Noske attempted nothing of the kind. He got in touch with General von Lüttwitz, a typical Prussian of the old order, and entrusted him and the frag-ments of the old army at his disposal with the task of suppressing the Spartacists. Lüttwitz carried out the task allotted to him with no great difficulty, for the Spartacists were very incompetent; he also took the law into his own hands and killed the Sparta-cist leaders without reference to the government.

It is curious to compare the situation in Germany at this date with that in Russia sixteen months earlier. In each we find the same ingredients: a fallen monarchy; a new and ramshackle Liberal govern-ment; leaders of fragments of the defeated army of the old régime, such as Kornilov and (at a later date) Denikin in Russia, or Lüttwitz in Germany; and lastly, small gangs of communist revolutionaries. Liberalism proved equally feeble in both countries, but in Russia the gift for leadership lay with the communists; in Germany it lay with the military men. The suppression of the Spartacists was supposed, at the time, to have confirmed the position of the Republic. It is now gauged more accurately as the first step in the 'counter-revolution' of which the last step was the accession of Hitler to power in 1933.

In February 1919 elections were held for a democratic national assembly which was to meet at Weimar and make the new republican constitution. For this and for subsequent elections under the new constitution the Germans adopted a system quite different from that which prevails in England and in most parliamentary countries. The voters did not vote in small constituencies for individual candidates, but in large provinces and for parties. Each party had a list of candidates. Suppose that in a given province there were a million voters, and a hundred members to be elected, and that there were four parties, A, B, C, and D, and that A party secured 500,000 votes, B 250,000, C 200,000 and D 50,000. Then the first fifty names on A's list would be elected, the first twenty-five on B's, the first twenty on C's, and the first five on D's.

This must seem very satisfactory to those who make a god of the multiplication table—rather a jejune religion, perhaps. But it is surely singular that those who pay us the compliment of imitating the parliamentary system which, after all, we invented, should confine their imitation to the merest generalities and should imagine that they could, by paper calculations, improve upon a system which we have arrived at by practice. The very first necessity of a democratic parliamentary system is that it should be *interesting*, and what is interesting to ordinary people is personal contest. Hence the popularity of games in England and of war in Germany. This element which can be provided by a political contest in a small area between known individuals is totally lacking to a contest in a large area between abstract parties. Another necessity is that the system should produce strong governments. For this a two-party system is better than a multiplication of groups, and it is far better that whichever side wins, by however small a margin of votes, should be given an effective majority than that the distribution of seats in the House should correspond exactly with the distribution of votes in the electorate. In all these respects the British system is good, and the Weimar constitution was bad. The Weimar constitution did not stifle German democracy at birth, for that unfortunate, or non-existent, infant was never born; but it contributed a few more nails to its coffin.[1]

The result of the elections for the Weimar Assembly was that in a House of 400 members only 185 were even nominally republican. The majority were monarchists at heart, who were prepared to make the best of republican institutions for the present. The government relied from the first on the services of the old Imperial civil service. Indeed, one of the most extraordinary features of the interlude of the Weimar republic is that the Imperial civil servants, including the teachers in the state schools and universities, survived the fall of the Imperial régime and carried on under its successor, which they despised. They were still there when Hitler

[1] A non-existent infant can perfectly well have a coffin—with nothing in it; in fact a cenotaph, or empty tomb.

E'

arrived, and they welcomed him. He was not quite
what they had expected, but he was an improvement
on 'Weimar'.

After making the constitution the Weimar
Assembly had to accept the Treaty of Versailles as
described in the first chapter of this book. The
severity of the terms created a genuine surprise.
The very men who, when they expected Germany
to win the war, had applauded projects which
would have crushed and mutilated all Germany's
neighbours, were filled with virtuous indignation
when forced to swallow a draught of the medicine
that they had intended to administer to others.
Englishmen, who are peculiarly ready to blame
themselves and their allies when things go wrong
with their enemies, often assumed during the next
few years that it was the Treaty of Versailles and
the occupation of the Ruhr four years later which
hardened the hearts of the Germans, and set them on
the road to revenge, but it was not so to any appre-
ciable extent. What set the Germans on the road to
revenge was neither Versailles nor the Ruhr occupation but the fact that they had been beaten. Still,
the fact that the Weimar government accepted the
Treaty was another nail in its coffin in the eyes of the
men of the old order. The fact that it was the men
of the old order who had made and lost the war
was not so much forgotten as 'explained' out of
existence.

During the last year of the war and the first year
after it the whole German people suffered seriously
from shortages of food and other necessities of life.
Naval blockade was one of the principal weapons of
war in the hands of their enemies and blockade

treats whole nations as besieging armies treat the
inhabitants of a besieged city. It tries to starve
them into surrender. Many Germans who glorified
war affected to regard the naval blockade as an
inhuman and unfair weapon—a typical piece of
German sentimentality. It might seem at first sight
that they were on stronger ground when they com-
plained of the continuance of the blockade for many
months after the armistice, and liberally disposed
British writers, with characteristic generosity and
perhaps characteristic inaccuracy, have supported
the German case on this point. But actually it was
almost entirely due to the choice of the German
Republican Government that the blockade was prolonged. In the terms of the armistice the allies
declared their intention of supplying Germany with
foodstuffs, but there were two limiting factors,
transport and finance. The armistice terms, unwisely perhaps, left Germany in possession of her
merchant shipping, amounting to about 1,000,000
tons, and her enormous gold reserve of £120,000,000,
more than twice as large as it had been at the beginning of the war. The Allies held that the Germans
must pay for their food, and pay in gold, and must
use their own shipping for its transport. Both these
demands were obviously reasonable and the German
Government refused to accede to either of them
until March 1919. As soon as they gave way, food
from the allied countries began to pour into Germany
and the blockade was in fact over, though it was
not technically terminated until the signature of the
Treaty of Versailles.

One may well ask why it was that the German
Government insisted on inflicting an extra four

months starvation on their own people. Apparently the shipping magnates held that they could make more money by employing their ships in other ways and the financiers, who were mostly men of the old régime, clung desperately to their gold reserve as a piece of salvage from the wreck of the war.

The true story of the post-war blockade is interesting because at no other point has German propaganda been so overwhelmingly successful in substituting the lie for the truth. Out of every thousand British persons who have heard or read the story (a perfectly true story, of course) of British soldiers in Cologne during the first months of 1919 filled with pity and indignation at the sight of starving German children and insisting on sharing their rations with them, it is probable that not more than one is aware that the continued starvation of these children was due not to the malice of the Allies but to the deliberate refusal of the proper facilities by the German Government.

As to the extent of the starvation inflicted, it is very difficult to arrive at an accurate estimate of German sufferings during these months. They were doubtless considerable though doubtless often exaggerated. We were told at the time that a whole generation of German children would grow up permanently enfeebled by their period of privation, but when, fifteen years later, these same children had grown to manhood, and were organized in Hitler's armies we were called upon to admire their magnificent physique. But perhaps the seeds of a permanent psychological damage had been sown by the famine.

In the spring of 1920 a group of monarchists of

the officer class, among them Lüttwitz, who had suppressed the Spartacists, made a premature and unsuccessful attempt to regain power. It is known as the Kapp Putsch—Putsch meaning much the same as the French *coup d'état*, a revolution by means of conspiracy and a sudden act of violence. Kapp and his associates seized Berlin. The government withdrew to Stuttgart and ordered a general strike of the workers. The workers responded and Kapp's position became impossible. He fled. Those of his associates who were captured were very leniently treated, for the government was afraid to offend its enemies.

In 1922 the German Government secured a conspicuous success in the diplomatic field—the Treaty of Rapallo with Russia. This treaty included a secret military arrangement of great value to Germany in her efforts to avoid the disarmament which had been imposed upon her. It was secretly arranged that, in return for an annual payment, selected German officers should be sent to Russia and trained in the handling of heavy artillery, tanks, and military aircraft, weapons which Germany was forbidden to possess. There was established a flying school for German officers outside Moscow. This arrangement continued until 1935, two years after Hitler had come into power. It was then brought to an end, nominally because Russia had made an alliance with France, but actually because German rearmament had progressed so far that Hitler no longer needed it. The author of the treaty on the German side was Walter Rathenau. Probably the two ablest ministers of the Weimar republic in its early years were Rathenau and Erzberger, both

Jews; they were both murdered by members of the old officer class.

The reparation demand and the occupation of the Ruhr were accompanied by the complete devaluation of the mark. In the end one mark or a million marks were equally worth just nothing at all. Every one who had savings invested in German institutions had those savings simply wiped out. If Germany had no political revolution in 1918 she can claim to have had an economic revolution in 1923. It seems roughly true to say that the inflation enriched the peasants and the landowners, who retained their land and were relieved of their debts. It also enriched a small class of expert financiers and capitalists, who may have been largely responsible for procuring the inflation and in any case knew how to turn it to their own advantage. It impoverished every one else. In enriching landowners and capitalists it enriched the enemies of the republic. Those whom it impoverished blamed the government and transferred their hopes for the future either to the Right, the monarchists and the old order, or to the Left, the communists.

It was during the occupation of the Ruhr, in November 1923, that Hitler first became visible to history. Ever since the end of the war he had been pursuing the career of an ultra-patriotic and anti-communist agitator. He had already founded his National-Socialist party, drawn up a programme for it, and conceived the idea, so congenial to the German mind, of putting his 'storm troops' into a uniform, the famous brown shirt. A certain von Kahr had recently established a transitory dictatorship in Munich. On November 8, while he was addressing an audience in the since famous Beer Hall, Hitler and his followers marched in to persuade him to lead an attack on Berlin, where Stresemann had just taken office. Von Kahr assented but changed his mind the next day. The Hitlerites thereupon staged a riot which was fired on by von Kahr's troops Hitler fled, but was captured and sentenced to five years' imprisonment. He was released after a few months, but while in prison he began the composition of his book, *Mein Kampf*. It is sometimes said that the Ruhr occupation poisoned Hitler's mind against France, but the most savage passages about France were written much later, at about the date of the Locarno Treaties. No one would remember the Hitler riot of 1923 to-day but for what happened later. It was an entirely trivial incident amid the riotous confusion of post-war Germany. A curious proof of this is that G. P. Gooch, one of the most learned authorities on post-war Germany, in his 400-page book on the subject, published in 1926, makes no mention of Hitler at all, and no reviewer of the book at the time of its publication called attention to his omission.

There followed the stabilization of the new German currency and the London Agreement accepting the Dawes Plan (1924), the Locarno Treaties (1925), Germany's admission to the League of Nations (1926), and the 'period of recovery' lasting down to the end of 1929. These subjects have been covered in the previous chapter.

In 1925, the year of Locarno, President Ebert died and a successor had to be elected. The Republicans put forward Dr. Marx, a respectable politician from their own ranks who, being the leader of the Catholic party, might well have drawn votes from the catholic section of the conservatives. The old order offered the aged Hindenburg, now close on his eightieth birthday, as an alternative. Apart from his military record, which had become a legend bearing little relation to facts, the old field-marshal was a representative of the East Prussian Junker (landowner) class who had feathered their own nests pretty successfully at the expense of other classes since the end of the war. Hindenburg was elected by a comfortable majority. There was also a left-wing revolutionary candidate, who polled only 2,000,000 votes out of the 30,000,000 cast. Those who voted for Hindenburg did not, of course, vote for National-Socialism, which most of them assuredly had never heard of. Still less did they vote in favour of another war; it is doubtful if they wanted this even in 1939. But they recorded a vote of no confidence in the Republic. It was the second step in the counter-revolution.

As for Stresemann, the predominant German statesman from his accession to office in 1923 to his death in 1929, he was hardly a democratic republican except for temporary convenience. Before and during the war he had been a Member of the National Liberal Party which, in earlier days, had provided Bismarck's firmest supporters from the establishment of the Empire onwards. He was still a member of the same party, though it had changed its name and called itself the German People's Party. By personal conviction he was a monarchist and throughout the years of his ministry he carried on a frank and confidential correspondence with the ex-Kaiser's eldest son, the heir to the empty German throne.

We now pass on into the shadows of the great slump, the central event and turning-point of our period, after which everything went wrong. 1930 was the first full year of the slump, and it is surely very interesting that in December of that year the phrase which has been taken as the title of this book was, prophetically, put into currency. Dr. Somary, a Swiss financier, lecturing at Chatham House in London during that month, declared that, unless effective steps were taken for the restoration of political confidence, 'the present crisis will be but a prelude to a dark period to which the historian of the future will give the name, "Between two Wars." '[1]

The great slump was not, of course, a merely German event, It did not even start in Germany. In America, where it started, it brought Franklin Roosevelt to the presidency, where he proceeded to fight it with his New Deal. In Britain it led to the formation of the MacDonald-Baldwin national government, and the abandonment of free trade. In the Far East it led Japan to invade Manchuria and to break away from the League of Nations. But it was in Germany that its consequences were most catastrophic.

What is a slump? It is the opposite of a boom, which is a period when society is full of optimism and confidence so far as money is concerned. Customers are prepared to buy on a large scale; the makers of goods are prepared to produce on a large scale

[1] G. M. Gathorne-Hardy, *A Short History of International Affairs, 1920–39*, p. 251.

because they feel confident of selling them; thus they build new factories, buy lots of their raw materials, employ more workers, pay good wages. Unemployment decreases towards vanishing-point. Shareholders profit as the value of their shares goes up. Money is abundantly borrowed and abundantly lent at high rates. Everybody's prosperity contributes to every one else's. Then comes a slump. Makers of goods have been too confident and have produced more than they can sell. They dismiss some of their employees. Speculators who have bought stocks at excessive prices become alarmed and sell on a falling market. The farther the boom has gone the more violent the reaction is likely to be. Bankruptcies abound. All confidence is lost. Then, after a number of lean years, the demand of the buyers begins to revive. the producer takes heart again, and so on. Some think that these unfortunate alternations are the result of 'the capitalist system' and would disappear if production was controlled by the State; but whether governments, who are so often politically foolish, would be economically wiser than private capitalists seems uncertain.

All through the nineteenth century booms and slumps had alternated. Throughout the war there had been, industrially, a tremendous boom, for governments were prepared to buy everything in the way of war material that could possibly be produced. After the war there was a brief continuance of the boom, due to the arrears of ordinary civilian demand that had accumulated during the war. This was followed by a very severe slump during the period 1921–3 the period of the failure of the first reparations settlement and the occupation of the

Ruhr. Then followed a boom period, 1923–9. America attained unprecedented wealth and prosperity, but no European country enjoyed a greater boom in those years than Germany.

Then came in the autumn of 1929 the beginning of such a slump as the world had never seen before. Its effects were most clearly seen in international trade. Between 1929 and 1933 the volume of the international trade of the world shrank till it was barely one-third of what it had been. Nothing like this had ever happened before. It was as much a record among slumps as the war of 1914–18 had been a record among wars. In Great Britain, which had never enjoyed the full tide of the boom, unemployment figures rose from one million to three. In Germany they rose from almost nothing to six millions.

What was the cause of the great slump? Was it some mysterious *malaise* traceable to the war now ten years distant? Such a vague explanation afforded no clue. Some pointed to the over-rapid mechanization of industry. Others pointed to tariffs. Never before had the states of the world done so much to discourage international trade by taxing what competed with the productions of their home markets. Others pointed to the chaos of currencies. Before 1914 all the currencies of the civilized world had fixed values in relation to one another, measured in gold. During the war every European currency had abandoned the gold standard, and the few which had since, like Great Britain, struggled back to the re-establishment of their old gold parity, seemed to have reason to regret it. The absence of fixed standards of foreign money values clearly added to the hazards of international trade.

All these causes, mechanization, tariffs, currency chaos, may have contributed to the slump of 1929 and made it worse, but they cannot be regarded as its cause, for all of them were features of the whole period since 1918. They do not account for a slump in 1929 following a six years' boom.

The slump began in Wall Street, New York, where the stock market collapsed after a period of mad gambling had driven the prices of shares up to fantastic heights. Americans had already before this begun to call back the short-term loans they had made to Germany in order to use the money more profitably in their own country. After the collapse of the American market they called it back more stridently. Germany could not find the money. Part of it had gone in paying reparations: part of it in capital expenditure, and was now stuck fast in bricks and mortar, ferro-concrete and machinery. In June 1931 the Credit-Anstalt, the principal bank of Austria, went bankrupt, and this caused a further 'run' on Germany, i.e. demands for repayment by Germany's creditors. In the mind of every German was the thought: 'this looks like 1923 over again when all our money went up in smoke. It simply must not happen a second time.' Communism was showing its head again. The republic and the parliamentary system were utterly discredited. A saviour was required, some one who would perform a miracle such as Napoleon had performed for France at the fag-end of the revolution, or Mussolini for Italy ten years back; and a saviour was already offering his services with all the resources of modern propaganda and modern gangsterism—Hitler.

A parallel and a contrast may be drawn between

the rise of Hitler to supreme power and the rise of
Napoleon. The contrast is obvious. Napoleon made
his name in a period of war by his dazzling victories
over his country's external enemies, Hitler in a
period of external peace and internal confusion by
self-advertisement and a vague but alluring programme of national regeneration and anti-Semitism.
The parallel lies in this. It was quite obvious, at the
end of the eighteenth century—Burke had forecast
it as early as 1791—that the French revolution would
end in a dictatorship, but it was not certain until the
last minute that Napoleon would be the dictator.
Sir John Seeley once wrote an interesting 'If' essay
showing how much better it would have been for the
French and for every one else if the dictatorship had
fallen to some more commonplace man. Similarly,
most people in Germany or outside it, refused to
believe till the very end that Hitler, the incomparable
agitator and author of confusion, would prove to be
the establisher of the new order. Was he not a mere
dreamer of dreams, a border-line case of insanity?
Almost to the last the men of the old order thought
they could use him as their tool. 'The people' might
believe in him, but 'the people' in Germany had
always been politically fools, and the governing
classes were accustomed to fooling them.

The figures polled by the Nazis[1] at successive
elections show the fortunes of the party during the
ten years before it came into power. In May 1924,
just before the Dawes Plan came into operation,
they polled nearly 2,000,000 votes and secured 32
seats in the Reichstag. In December 1924, when

[1] 'Nazi' is simply the first two syllables of National as
pronounced in German.

Stresemann's policy was beginning to justify itself, 900,000 votes and only 14 seats. In 1930, when the slump was already deepening, 6,400,000 votes and 107 seats. In July 1932, 13,700,000 votes and 230 seats. In November of the same year, 11,700,000 votes and 196 seats—a slight setback. In March 1933, after Hindenburg had already appointed Hitler Chancellor, 17,300,000 votes and 288 seats. Even this was less than half the Reichstag with its 646 seats, but some other parties allied with Hitler gave him a clear majority, and he used it to bring government by Reichstag and republican methods to an end. At his bidding the Reichstag committed suicide and entrusted him with a four-years' dictatorship.

In 1932, Brüning, the last German chancellor to owe his appointment to a parliamentary majority, was struggling with the problems of the slump and its six millions unemployed. He was trying to pursue the same policy as had been adopted by the new National Government in Great Britain, drastic increases in taxation and reductions in the pay of all government employees, a bleak policy which the British electorate had none the less endorsed by giving the National Government an overwhelming majority. Brüning's 'starvation government', as it was called, was intensely unpopular. Failing to get his measures through the Reichstag, he got Hindenburg's permission to issue them as emergency decrees, a course of action allowed by the terms of the Weimar constitution. The vast numbers of the unemployed had swelled the ranks both of the Nazi storm troopers ('Brownshirts') and the less disciplined ranks of the communists. These rebel armies, for such they were, rioted in protest against the decrees. Hindenburg dismissed Brüning and gave the chancellorship to Papen, a man of the old aristocracy, who formed a 'cabinet of barons'. Papen offered the vice-chancellorship to Hitler, who refused it, regarding the offer as a bribe and as a sign of weakness in his rival. The elections which followed, July 1932, raised Hitler's party in the Reichstag from 107 to 230. His henchman, Göring, was elected president of the House, which was almost immediately dissolved.

Papen resigned the chancellorship, and Hindenburg offered it to Hitler, on condition that he would include members of other parties in his cabinet. He refused. Another phantom chancellor, Schleicher, flitted across the scene, but was gone by the end of the year. In January 1933, though he had only 196 supporters in the new Reichstag, Hitler was offered the chancellorship without conditions, and accepted it. There seems no doubt that the men of the old order, who manipulated the actions of the aged puppet, Hindenburg, did not conceive that they were throwing up the sponge by this course of action. They felt confident that high office would expose the inadequacy of this strange fanatic, and that they were taking a course of action which would effectively prick the Nazi bubble. They were mistaken.

Hitler's agents at once took charge of Germany. The Reichstag was again dissolved and elections fixed for 5 March. A week before that date the Reichstag building was burnt down, presumably by Nazi agents, but the crime was attributed to the communists, and their leaders were at once arrested; for the communists and not the liberal parliamentarians were Hitler's most formidable rivals, though it was part of his propaganda to magnify their strength. He claimed to be delivering Germany not only from the proven inefficiency of the republicans, but also from the red ruin threatened by the communists.

What followed has already been told. The elections gave the Nazis and their allies a majority, and this majority gave Hitler his dictatorship. Hindenburg died a year later, and Hitler became president as well as chancellor; but it made little difference; he was already Führer, 'Leader', enjoying more absolute power than any previous ruler of Germany.

One of Hitler's first acts was to appoint Goebbels minister of propaganda, a post for which he was perfectly fitted and continued to hold until the régime was overwhelmed by the Allied invasion twelve years later. There followed a series of decrees. One of them abolished at a stroke the semi-independent governments of all the states—Prussia, Bavaria and the rest—that had combined to make Bismarck's empire, and had survived under the Weimar constitution. A second abolished all rival party organizations; henceforth a German was either a Nazi or a traitor in danger of a concentration camp. A third was directed against the rights and privileges of great non-political corporations, such as churches and trade unions; a German was allowed only one loyalty—to Hitler. A fourth was directed against Jews, and began what in a few years was to become the most hideous persecution in all the records of history. For the present Jews were merely excluded from all forms of government service, and under the term 'Jew' were included all who had married Jewesses, or had a Jewish parent or grand-parent. This is not the place to discuss the tragedy of the Jewish race or the problems involved in the history and psychology of anti-Semitism. It is a very complicated subject for which we have no space. Suffice it to say—what is obvious—that Hitler did not invent anti-Semitism; he found it ready to hand as one of the most attractive features in a programme which exalted the Germans as potentially the master-race of the world.

Hitler had thus established his dictatorship, but he had not yet secured absolute mastery within his own party. He had owed his majority in the last Reichstag to a coalition with another party, the so-called Nationalists, conservatives who represented big business interests and believed that they could use Hitler as a sort of propaganda agency for their own policy. They were soon rudely awakened from this dream. Their leader, Hugenberg, disappeared, and the party was amalgamated with the Nazi organization. There were also a few military men who had supported Hitler with the intention of using him in the same way. They too were gradually eliminated.

Finally and much more formidable, there was the revolutionary and socialist wing of Hitler's own party, led by Röhm. These men had played leading parts in creating the Brownshirt rebel army of Storm troopers (S.A.) which had lifted Hitler to power. They had aims irreconcilable with those of the officers of the regular army, whose support would henceforth be necessary to Hitler as the instruments of his programme of the rearmament of Germany. In fact he had to choose between his old

friends and his new ones, and he chose the latter.
Röhm and his party were destroyed in the blood
purge, organized by Göring, of 30 June 1934. It was
a *coup d'état* of astonishing dimensions. Something
like a thousand people were murdered by Nazi
agents, many of the murdered being, apparently, the
victims of private and personal feuds within the Nazi
organization. So the revolutionary Brownshirts
(S.A.) were liquidated and succeeded by the authori-
tarian Black Guards (S.S.), controlled first by Göring
and afterwards by Himmler.

A curious illustration of the failure of average
intelligent opinion in England to foresee the future
may be found in *The Times* editorial comment on
this 'blood bath'. 'In the next years there is more
reason to fear for Germany than to fear Germany.'
No doubt the same sort of comment was made by
the same sort of people regarding France during the
Robespierrian Terror, when Napoleon was an obscure
major of artillery. In Germany the Robespierre of
1934 and the Napoleon of 1940 were one and the
same person.

THE SUCCESSION STATES

'The Succession States' was a term which came
into common use to describe the new states formed
out of the old Austro-Hungarian Empire. It is here
used in the widest sense to cover all the states,
except Italy, which possess any territory which used
to form part of that Empire. We can afford no more
than a brief glance at each of them.

The Austrian republic was the German-populated
part of the old Empire, what was left when everything else had been taken away. Its economic

prospects were grim from the first to last. Its demand for union with Germany was refused even before the peace conference met, and it never succeeded in establishing with its new neighbours the degree of freedom of trade essential to its well-being. In 1919 the victorious Allies, instead of demanding reparations from it, found themselves impelled to come to its financial assistance. A series of relief measures culminated in a drastic scheme of reconstruction put forward by the Financial Committee of the League, and adopted in October 1922. Under this scheme loans to Austria were guaranteed by Britain, France, Italy, Czechoslovakia, and several other states, and the guarantors formed a committee of control under a Dutch president to supervise Austrian finances. It worked well for several years.

Like Germany, Austria began her post-war existence as a parliamentary republic, but Fascist opposition developed from 1927 onwards, and in 1933 a Fascist dictatorship was established under Dollfuss. In 1931 Austria, at the instigation of Brüning, the German chancellor at that time, had asked permission of the League to make a customs union with Germany, a project vetoed by France, but in view of the Nazi menace to Austrian independence Dollfuss preferred to put his trust in what eventually proved the broken reed of Mussolini. His position was a very weak one, for he was as it were between the devil and the deep sea; on one side Hitlerite Germany, on the other the Viennese socialist party. In February 1934 he opened a ferocious attack, with tanks and machine-guns, on the socialist headquarters in Vienna. In June of the same year

Austrian Nazi exiles were enabled by Hitler to invade the country from Bavaria, and Dollfuss was murdered.

A good deal of mystery surrounds the sequel to these events. Mussolini moved troops up to the Austrian frontier and it may be that, as Mr. Harold Butler says, 'Hitler's courage failed him at the last moment and the expected German aid was withheld'. The absorption of Austria into the Reich was thus postponed from 1934 to 1938. Another Austrian dictator, Schuschnigg, succeeded to Dollfuss's position and pursued the same precarious policy.

The old Austria-Hungary, ever since the successful Magyar ultimatum of 1867 addressed to a Habsburg government which had just suffered defeat at the hands of Prussia, had consisted of two states separate in all respects except that they had the same monarch and the same foreign policy. Their relationship was, in fact, like that of England and Scotland from the accession of James I to the Act of Union. In Austria the government had been a mild despotism, in Hungary an oppressive oligarchy of the Magyar landowners. Post-war Hungary was no worse off than post-war Austria, but she accepted her lot much less patiently. She refused to accept the fact that the Habsburg dynasty, once her oppressor, but for the last fifty years her tool, could no longer be allowed to reign, and she symbolized her defiance of this fact by entitling her ruler, not president, as of a republic, but 'regent', acting on behalf of a non-existent king. She hoped some day to recover lost territories from Rumania, Jugoslavia and Czechoslavakia, and was, for some reason or other, encouraged to cherish these ambitions by an irresponsible but powerful English press magnate, Lord Rothermere.

Czechoslovakia was much the most highly civilized and industrialized of the small states of central Europe, and the only state east of Switzerland to preserve a genuinely democratic and parliamentary system of government right down to the end of its independent existence in 1938. Yet it laboured under great natural difficulties. Its extremely long, narrow shape is suggestive of an artificial creation, and its larger western end was surrounded on three sides by potentially hostile Germans. Moreover, Germans overlapped its frontiers, and the 3,000,000 Sudeten Germans, as they were called, made up one-fifth of its total population. Seven and a half million Czechs shared with the Germans the ancient kingdom of Bohemia. Farther east, in Slovakia and Ruthenia, were two and a half million Slovaks, well over half a million Magyars, over half a million Ruthenes, and 80,000 Poles. The total is just over fourteen millions, so that the Czechs made up scarcely more than half the population, unless the Slovaks were regarded as one with them. But the Czechs were an industrial population with a culture reaching back to the fourteenth century when, under their national hero, Huss, they wrestled with the Germans for the control of the University of Prague, whereas the Slovaks were for the most part primitive peasants long subjected to the oppressive domination of the Magyars. Perhaps the union of the Czechs and Slovaks was facilitated by the fact that the creation of an independent Czechoslovakia was very largely the work of Masaryk, a noble-minded old man who was himself a Slovak. He was president of the republic up to his death, for more than half the term of its existence between the wars. Certainly the Czechoslovak state gave equal representation to all its national groups in its parliament, and it was for many years commonly quoted as the most successful and best conducted of all the new states produced by the war.

The great slump hit Czechoslovakia hard, and the blow fell most severely on the Sudeten German districts. Not only were they the most industrialized, but many of their industries, such as textiles, glass and china, were more sensitive to depression than such Czech industries as boots, beer, and armaments, all of which seem to be regarded as 'necessities'. The closing of the German frontier against exports from Czechoslovakia hit them hard, and the Sudeten Germans, instead of blaming Germany for this policy, grumbled because the Czech Government did not do more for their relief. However, there was hardly any demand among the Sudetens for incorporation in the Reich until their leader, Henlein, was persuaded to make himself the mouthpiece of Hitler's expansionist policy.

In Jugoslavia the non-Slav minorities are fortunately small, but the country from the first suffered from the tension between its Slavic units, which was much severer than the tension between Czechs and Slovaks, because their strength was much more evenly balanced. In Czechoslovakia numbers, wealth, culture, and possession of the capital were all on the side of the Czechs as against the Slovaks. In Jugoslavia these assets were distributed. The Serbs possessed the slight superiority in numbers, the capital, and the prestige of independence throughout a hundred years of somewhat unedifying history, but the Croats and the Slovenes (who may be taken together, though they speak different languages) were much more civilized. The very nature of the new state was a subject of contention. The Croats and the Slovenes desired a federal union of three self-governing communities; the Serbs desired, and secured, a united kingdom of 'Southern Slavs' (Jugoslavia). The three peoples were prepared to present a united front to Italian aggression, but they could agree on little else. The early history of Jugoslavia was turbulent and bloodstained, culminating in a parliamentary incident in 1928 when a Serb member rose in the House and, instead of making a speech, drew a revolver and picked off one member after another of the Croat opposition. After this, King Alexander suppressed parliamentary government and established a royal dictatorship. In 1934 he was murdered at Marseilles by Croat assassins.

The problem of Rumania resembled that of Jugoslavia to this extent, that an insignificant and backward Balkan state more than doubled its size by the acquisition of populations accustomed to the much more highly civilized standards of the old Habsburg Empire. Thus there was tension not only between the idle and corrupt government of Bucharest and the non-Rumanian peoples in the new provinces, the Magyars being the most important, but also between the government and the Rumanians of the newly acquired provinces. The new Rumania had bitten off more than she could chew. She was almost bound some day to lose Bessarabia to Russia, and she would be lucky if she did not lose a large part of Transylvania and the other newly acquired western provinces to Hungary.

A good deal has already been said about the beginnings of the new Poland, the complication of her frontier with Germany and her successful aggression eastwards at the expense of both Lithuania and Russia. Politically the Poles have always been notorious for their incompetence, and the early history of the new Poland showed that in this respect the Poles had unfortunately not changed their character. Pilsudski, a very remarkable man, had been the principal creator fo the new Poland and became Head of the State, but in 1921 he insisted on retiring. After his retirement the parliamentary system worked more inefficiently than ever, and in 1926 he re-emerged and established a dictatorship, which he retained until his death ten years later.

If Rumania was wedged between Russia and Hungary, Poland was in the even more perilous predicament of being wedged between Russia and Germany. Both were down and out in 1919, but both were bound to recover some day, and both of them would then have old scores to pay off. In these circumstances Poland put her trust in a French alliance, and by the 'eastern' Locarno treaty of 1925 France undertook to support Poland in case of German attack. But was the French guarantee of much value? Pilsudski came to doubt it, and in January 1934 the world was surprised to hear that he had signed a ten years' pact with Hitler, both parties renouncing the use of force in the settlement of their problems for that space of time. At the same time France was feeling her way towards an alliance with Russia.

Lloyd George once described the old Austro-Hungary as a ramshackle empire. The same term is equally or even more applicable to all the states which had sprung up on the site of its ruins. Each of these states had its own sources of weakness and in no two cases quite the same, but over and above their special weaknesses they all suffered from their newness. There was a certain artificiality about them. They were 'half baked'. With time the newness might have worn off, the more pressing problems might have been solved, and a stability, such as old countries take for granted, secured: but time was what they were not allowed.

FRANCE

In November 1918 France was in the position of one who has, at appalling cost, attained the goal of his desires but is terribly afraid that he will not be able to retain what he has for the moment secured. The war had proved that an alliance of almost all the great powers could beat Germany; yes, but it had also proved that Germany was immeasurably more powerful than France. Such a war must never come again; France could not face it. It was such a state of mind, rather than a spirit of triumphant vindictiveness, which caused whatever seemed to her more happily placed allies unreasonable in French policy towards Germany at the Peace Conference and during the years that followed.

The most conspicuous fact on the morrow of the armistice was the devastation of the northern departments. One-tenth of France was utterly laid waste, having provided for four years the principal battle area of the war. The French set to work at once to restore and rebuild, without much regard for economy. Where did the money come from? At the moment from loans. In the end *les Boches paieront*— or so it was hoped. Germany must find the money for repairing the damage she had done to the chief industrial district of France. To the average French-man the word 'reparations', which to an Englishman vaguely suggests compensations, meant simply what it means outside any French motor garage—repairs. Actually Germany never paid for more than a small fraction of the damage she had done, and the French taxpayer was not very ready to pay for it either. One of the curious differences between the English and the French is that, while the English pay very heavy taxes with remarkable willingness and honesty, but have hitherto shown an extreme reluctance to submit to conscription except actually during a war, the French accept conscription as a matter of course, but regard high taxation as intolerable. The result was that, during the period between the wars, France hardly ever balanced her budget. Governments, especially governments of the 'Left' or progressive parties, did not dare to impose the taxes that the financial position required, and the taxes that were imposed were largely evaded.

The end of tne war found France in a state of inevitable dislocation and unrest. Would France go the way of Russia and plunge into red revolution? There were many who feared it. Indeed, those who feared it proved to be far more numerous than those who hoped for it; for the first post-war general election, in November 1919, returned the biggest Conservative majority since the foundation of the republic. The *bloc national* came into power.[1] One of the first duties of the new Chamber was to elect a president in place of Poincaré, whose seven-year term was ending. Clemenceau was passed over in favour of Deschanel, an obscure politician who subsequently went mad and was replaced by an extreme conservative, Millerand. I have said earlier that Clemenceau was passed over because he refused to put the popular demand for the Rhine frontier before the Peace Conference, but it is doubtless true that his over-strong character and his anti-religious opinions also told against him. The former would tell against him in all French parliaments called on to elect a president, the latter in a parliament with a strong conservative bias.

So the old game of French politics, as played according to the rules and conventions of the Third Republic, got going again, in so far as it had ever stopped during the war. The French Revolution may have conferred great benefits on France, but it has inflicted on her one hitherto irreparable injury. Since that upheaval, now a hundred and fifty years old, no type of constitution has won the allegiance of the French nation as a whole. The restored monarchy, the Orleans monarchy, the Second Empire, the republic, all of them have alienated one-half of France. France had become a republic after the defeat of 1870, much as Germany had become a republic after the defeat of 1918, not because she

[1] The words, *bloc, front* and *cartel* are used in French politics to denote combinations of the numerous and small political parties into which the country is divided.

wanted to be a republic, but because there seemed nothing else to do. The republic was regarded with contempt by some of the best sections of French society, who simply stood aloof from its activities. Among these classes were the Catholic church and the army officer class. French republican politicians were not representatives of the whole of France, nor of the best of it.

There was little in the proceedings of French politics during the previous fifty years to reconcile to the republic those who regretted its establishment. Scandal had followed scandal. The rules of the game favoured jobbery and intrigue. The essential rule or custom of the constitution, for it was a matter of custom not of law, may be regarded as an unhappy compromise between the British and American rules. In Britain, parliament can dismiss a government, but a government can, when defeated, dissolve parliament and appeal to the electorate to decide between them. In America neither can get rid of the other: both president and congress are assured of the whole of their legal term of existence. In France the parliament could dismiss a government, but a government could not dissolve parliament; it was secure within its four years' legal term. The result was that the parliament enjoyed itself and wasted its time playing political ninepins, knocking down one government and setting up another, a game facilitated by the fact that no government ever enjoyed a majority consisting of a single homogeneous party, but was always what Burke called a coalition government of his own day, 'a tessellated pavement without cement', an uneasy and treacherous alliance of little groups of ministers, each with

their own little party following and their own
ambitions.

The leading figures in French politics up to 1930
were Aristide Briand and Raymond Poincaré.
Briand was, as we have seen, a man of a generous
international outlook; Poincaré a narrow and austere
nationalist. Briand was a most delightful and
amusing man, and his humorous remarks enlivened
many international conferences. Foreigners did not
find Poincaré either amusing or delightful, but they
found him a formidable adversary. In 1921 Briand
was prime minister. In January 1922, at a conference
of allied statesmen at Cannes, he nearly succeeded in
securing from Lloyd George a renewal of the British
guarantee to support France if attacked by Germany,
in return for certain French concessions in the sharing
out of reparation payments; but his colleagues were
not prepared for these concessions, and Briand was
dismissed by President Millerand. Poincaré took his
place, and was responsible a year later for the French
occupation of the Ruhr.

The second peace-time general election took place
early in 1924 and, coming after the admitted failure
of the Ruhr venture and the general discredit of
Poincaré's policy, gave a majority to the *cartel gauche*,
a combination of so-called radicals and socialists.
Herriot became prime minister and, with Ramsay
MacDonald, was responsible for the London Agreement, accepting the Dawes Plan for the payment of
reparations, which was followed by the Locarno
treaties.

But though the radicals rendered great service in
the matter of Franco-German relations, they showed
neither skill nor courage in finance. The franc began

to lose value alarmingly in relation to the pound and the dollar. Herriot fell, and a bewildering succession of ministers followed one another, each lasting a few weeks. Popular opinion looked to Poincaré as a man who would not be afraid to administer unpleasant medicine to his country when required. In fact the parliament that had been elected to get rid of him now gave him its confidence. So, having failed in 1923 to get the money France needed out of Germany, he had now, in 1926, to get it out of France, or rather out of the French taxpayer. There followed what was undoubtedly the most prosperous period in recent French history, the years we have already described as the 'period of recovery', 1926–9. Poincaré saved the franc, and held the premiership for the unusually long period (in France) of three years. Briand, formerly his rival, was now his foreign secretary, and as such welcomed Germany to the League of Nations. The general election of 1928 took the form of an emphatic vote of confidence in these two statesmen.

One of the troubles of these years was presented by the problems of Alsace. The restoration of Alsace to France had been, as a matter of sentiment, a cherished ambition of patriotic Frenchmen ever since its loss in 1871. Ever since that date, down to 1918, the seated figure representing Strasbourg in the Place de la Concorde, the Trafalgar Square of Paris, had been draped in mourning robes. But the best of friends, if parted for fifty years, find that they have drifted apart, and the Alsatians did not find the French republican régime, which allowed them much less local liberty than the German imperial system had done, at all congenial. The Alsatians were strongly Catholic and dominated by their priests, and resented the secularizing of their state schools. The point is introduced here merely to illustrate the fact that alterations of frontier and allegiance, however well justified, involve difficulties of adjustment. No transfer of territory made by the Peace Conference was more entirely justified than that of Alsace. If even here the new shoe pinched, one can multiply the Alsatian problem by a hundred and get some faint idea of the maladjustments prevailing all over the map of the new Europe.

The Minister of War in Poincaré's Cabinet was Maginot, and he began making the famous 'line', or system of defences, that bore his name. This was in fact a preparation for the future, when the Allied garrisons would be withdrawn from the Rhineland. One of the three sections of the Rhineland had been evacuated in 1926. The others were due for evacuation in 1930 and 1935, but actually both were evacuated, as a wholly unappreciated gesture of goodwill, in 1930. In part, however, the Maginot line was intended to compensate for the fact that France at the same time reduced the period of conscript service from eighteen to twelve months, for reasons of economy and to satisfy popular demand. The line protected, or was meant to protect, the whole Franco-German frontier, but it did not cover the longer Belgium frontier through which the Germans had come in 1914. It was a half-hearted undertaking.

Poincaré resigned on account of ill-health in 1929 and retired to his native Lorraine to die. It is said that he used to look through his eastern windows towards the German frontier and murmur, 'they will come again'. Briand lingered on a year or two at the foreign office, but his work of conciliation was done, so far as he could do it, and he had a premonition that it would prove a failure.

France suffered less directly, at any rate at first, from the great slump than either Britain or Germany, for the slump was felt most severely in international trade, and France depended less on exports than her more industrialized neighbours. But indirectly it affected her at once. In 1930 President Hoover of the United States proposed a one year's moratorium of all reparation and inter-allied debt payments. The French resented this. They felt that it was an American device for securing the repayment from Germany of her own commercial loans in preference to reparation payments due to France. They also foresaw that, though the moratorium was nominally for a year, reparation payments would never be renewed—as was in fact agreed at the Lausanne conference in 1932. When, in spite of the cessation of reparation payments, America demanded the resumption of the payment of war-debt instalments due to herself, France felt she had been tricked and bluntly refused to pay.

The general election of 1932 gave a substantial majority to the parties of the Left, and the internal history of France during the next four years was to be, in essentials, a repetition of that of 1924-8. On each occasion the parties of the Left secured a majority, but soon got themselves into such financial trouble that they had to make way for a 'national' government representing both Right and Left parties—in the earlier period the government of Poincaré, in the later period the government of

Doumergue, followed by that of Laval. But in the earlier period the European situation was steadily improving and the national government of Poincaré, with Briand at the foreign office, had been a success. In the latter period Hitler rose to power in Germany and the European situation got steadily worse.

The misfortunes of the numerous and ephemeral Left-wing government of 1932–4—there were about a dozen of them—were in part due to the fact that French finances, and with them the international standing of the franc, were once again in a critical condition. In part they were due to the Stavisky scandal. Stavisky was a Russian-Jewish swindler, long resident in France, who committed suicide to avoid capture by the police in January 1934. It soon became known that he had been arrested on a serious charge seven years before, but had been released without trial and the case against him dropped. High officials and well-known politicians, including Chautemps, who was prime minister at the time of Stavisky's death, were accused of being responsible for the fact that this criminal had been allowed to escape punishment and to repeat his offences. It was, indeed, widely asserted and believed that Stavisky had been 'suicided' by the police in order to hush up the revelations that would have resulted from his trial.

These facts and suspicions gave an opening to all those who disliked and despised the whole system of republican government. There were the royalists, still on active opposition, though scarcely hoping for a restoration of monarchy. Their paper, *Action Française*, was widely read on account of the brilliantly scurrilous and amusing articles of Léon

F

Daudet. There was the Croix de Feu, the French fascist organization. Chautemps resigned, and his colleague Daladier took his place. There were riots led by the Croix de Feu outside the Chamber of Deputies on 6 February, followed by a counter-demonstration by the communists on 9 February, and a one-day general strike organized by the socialists as an anti-fascist demonstration on 12 February. It looked as if France might be sinking into·anarchy, to be followed by some kind of dicta-torship, as Italy had done in 1922. And these things happened a year after Hitler had come into power in Germany.

Salvation was sought in the appointment as prime minister of an elderly statesman who had been president from 1924 to 1931 and now regarded him-self as outside party politics—Doumergue. On becoming prime minister he set up commissions of inquiry in the Stavisky scandal and the recent riots. The inquiries revealed a great deal of inefficiency and a good deal of corruption, but very few of those found in fault were made to suffer. He also tried to persuade the French parliament to remodel its pro-cedure on English lines: more particularly to allow the president to dissolve the chambers on the advice of the prime minister, but his proposals were given no serious consideration.

Doumergue's foreign minister, Barthou, opened negotiations which were intended to combine Russia and Italy and the states of the 'little entente'—Czechoslovakia, Jugoslavia, and Rumania—in oppo-sition to Nazi aggression. In the course of these negotiations King Alexander of Jugoslavia visited France and was met by Barthou at Marseilles, where they were both assassinated by a Croatian fanatic who resented the king's dictatorship. Barthou, a man of the old generation who had been prime minister before the first great war, was the last French statesman before 1939 to show courage and initiative in foreign policy. He was succeeded by the afterwards notorious Laval, who dominated French politics throughout 1935, first as foreign minister, and afterwards as prime minister. He made an effort to conciliate Germany and also to secure that, if Germany could not be conciliated, Italy would be on the side of France. We shall encounter him and his 1935 foreign policy again in the next chapter.

Early in 1936 Hitler denounced the Treaty of Locarno, and sent his troops into the demilitarized Rhineland. One might have thought that this shattering event would have drawn all French parties together in a common patriotism. But there was something wrong with France, and the challenge provoked no healthy reaction. The French elections, which were held a month later in accordance with the normal quadrennial routine, turned almost entirely on party rivalries. The parties of the Left felt that, owing to Stavisky and to one thing and another, they had been cheated of the fruits of the electoral victory they had won four years earlier. They now combined their electioneering efforts in an organization called *le front populaire*, and the most popular item in their programme was the destruction of the French fascist 'armies' as a menace to democracy. They were doubtless helped by the fact that a few weeks before the elections some fascist gangsters had made a murderous attack on Léon Blum, the leader of the socialist party. In any case the *front populaire* won a sweeping victory, and Blum, as leader of the largest party in the coalition, became prime minister. He was a highly cultured Jew, admired for the elegant style of his oratory and his journalism, but without the force of character to cope with a crisis. Another result of the elections was to raise the number of communist deputies from ten to seventy-two. The communists were outside the *front populaire* and were, of course, as anti-republican as the fascists.

The victory of the *front populaire* was followed by widespread strikes, designed perhaps to ensure that the politicians fulfilled without delay their electoral promises to the industrial workers. The new government responded by limiting the hours of work in mines and factories to a forty-hour week—this at a moment when France was supposed to be feverishly rearming in an effort to keep abreast of the rearmament of Germany, where men were working seventy hours a week or more. At the same time, the advent to power of the *front populaire*, with its Jewish leader, undoubtedly increased the depth of the schism dividing France into those who supported the republic and those who opposed it, thus further disintegrating the national will. From the standpoint of the oncoming German menace it was a disaster.

France had, in fact, several years before the war broke out, become 'the sick man of Europe'—or one of them.

GREAT BRITAIN

The nations whose histories we have thus far reviewed all of them continued throughout the period to be obsessed either by the consequences of the war or by the consequences of revolutionary movements which had grown out of it. When we cross the Channel, still more when we cross the Atlantic, we reach communities which regarded the war as a thing of the past and were very ready to forget all about it, if only 'foreigners' would allow them to do so. The British and the Americans had their own sound traditions, and were very well able to look after themselves. As Cincinnatus returned to his plough directly he had finished the little job of politics to which he was called as dictator, so the British and the Americans prepared themselves to resume their ordinary national lives, their ordinary history.

Certainly the British had plenty of objects of interest to draw their eyes away from the continent of Europe. The perennial Irish question had been at one of its recurrent boiling-points in July 1914. It was then successfully placed in cold storage, but less than two years later it escaped from the refrigerator and staged an Easter-week rebellion, 1916. After that things went from bad to worse. The enormous Conservative majority elected to support Lloyd George after the Armistice provided the very worst possible House of Commons for handling the problem of the Irish rebels who, after all, only wanted for themselves the sort of thing that the peace conference had been handing out wholesale to Czechs and Groats and Letts and Finns. Lloyd George, as a Welsh Protestant, never directed the dynamics of his political imagination to the problem of the Irish Catholics until compelled to do so by the mounting tide of Irish atrocities. When he did so, the result was the truce of 1921 and the eventual establishment of the Irish Free State. This arrangement may have benefited the Irish who clamoured for it. It has certainly proved an inestimable boon, except in times of war, to the British who were most reluctant to grant it, for it has got the Irish question out of British politics. There remains, of course, the frontier question, for Eire, as she now prefers to be called, is not content without Northern Ireland; but Northern Ireland, apart from two small and thinly populated border counties to which Eire seems to have a valid claim,[1] prefers to remain a self-governing unit within the United Kingdom.

Then there was the question of Egypt, which the maps of the previous thirty years had painted pink as no one knew whether it was part of the British Empire or not. It was a question of how you defined 'British Empire'. After the armistice the Egyptians violently indicated a preference for the latter view, and after an unedifying display of obstinacy, the British Government gave way. In 1922 Egypt became independent and at once, as a condition of its independence, negotiated a treaty with Britain which authorized the maintenance of a contingent of the British Army in Egypt, an arrangement for which the Egyptians had reason to be grateful when confronted with the prospect of Italian invasion in 1940. Here also there was a frontier question, for Egypt claimed the Sudan, but did not get it.

Thirdly, there was the problem of India, a terrible

[1] These two counties, Tyrone and Fermanagh, elect an Irish Republican member of the British parliament. He records his views in silence by refusing to take his seat.

problem which was not settled as easily as the problems of Ireland and Egypt, and indeed it is not settled yet. Beginning, so far as our period is concerned, with the Amritsar massacre, where a British general suppressed a revolutionary mob with a degree of bloodshed which caused a sharp division of opinion in England, the Indian question continued to trouble British politics. Two radical reforms of the whole system of government were introduced, the Montagu-Chelmsford reforms embodied in the Act of 1919, and the Indian Constitution of Sir Samuel Hoare's Act of 1935. But more, much more, seems to be required.

Besides these external problems there was grave industrial unrest, demands for better wages backed by a deep-seated dissatisfaction with the whole capitalist system. Never had there been such extensive and prolonged strikes as in the period 1919–26. The coal industry was the blackest spot. This industry is our industrial Ireland. The British believe that they have exceptional gifts for government, but admit that they always made a mess of governing Ireland. Similarly they believe that they have exceptional talents for industry, but they agree that their coal industry is the most inefficient in the world. Some blame the miners, others the mine-owners, and each of these blame the other. Indeed, they remind the impartial onlookers of the rival emperors in Tacitus's *Histories*, who accused each other of every crime in the calendar, *neuter falso*; 'neither of them falsely'. The faults of the miners and the mine-owners were not, to be sure, of the scandalous and fruity character of the vices attributed each to the other by these Roman emperors, but they were disastrous to the industry. That being so, should not the whole industry be nationalized and administered by the state? But how was this to be organized? And would not the remedy prove worse than the disease?

There was a miners' strike in the spring of 1919, and Mr. Justice Sankey's report on the industry for a time divided attention not unequally with the proceedings of the peace conference. There was another in 1921, which nearly involved a general strike, and a third in 1926 which actually did so. The general strike only lasted nine days and proved a complete failure, and on the whole the event raised British prestige in the eyes of the world. Here was the British revolution, or an attempt at it, for A. J. Cook, the miners' leader who very cleverly manœuvred the Trade Union Council into declaring the general strike, had described himself as 'a humble follower of Lenin'. Yet everything was as calm and orderly as a Victorian Sunday morning— or nearly so. In some districts the general strikers occupied their leisure in playing football matches with the special constables who had been enrolled to keep them in order.

Up to the date of the armistice Lloyd George had been the little Welsh wizard who won the war, but, once he had capitalized his immense reputation in the form of the overwhelming majority given him by the general election immediately afterwards, his wizardry seemed to fail him. Henceforth he appeared to be no better than a blundering opportunist. Politically he was a Liberal who had quarrelled with his party and was now kept in office by the Conservatives. In the autumn of 1922 the Conservatives came to the conclusion that he was more of a liability than an asset, and broke away from him. The general election which followed returned a Conservative majority, and Lloyd George's career in office was over, as it turned out, for ever. Bonar Law became prime minister, retiring six months later on grounds of health and giving place to Stanley Baldwin.

Baldwin and MacDonald shared the premiership between them throughout all the middle years of our period from 1923 to 1937. Baldwin gave place to MacDonald in January 1924, but succeeded him again before the end of the year, holding office till 1929. It was then MacDonald's turn again, but two years later the crisis of the great slump led to the formation of a National Government in which, though MacDonald was prime minister, Baldwin as the leader of far the largest group of supporters of the government was at least his equal in power and responsibility. MacDonald retired on account of failing health in 1935, once again making way for Baldwin, who retired for the same reason in 1937, and was succeeded by Neville Chamberlain. In our judgment of these two men is necessarily involved our judgment of British statesmanship throughout three-quarters of the period between the two wars, from just before the Dawes Plan till after the remilitarization of the Rhineland.

MacDonald was by party label a Labour man, but it is difficult to imagine anything more remote either from the British workman or the trade union boss than this studious, cultured, and romantic Highlander. The entirely baseless legend that, though born in a peasant's cottage, he was the illegitimate son of a Scottish nobleman suggests the impression that he created. His socialism was a youthful ardour which amounted to very little by the time he reached the premiership. His special interest by that time was international relations, which he approached in the spirit of Gladstonian idealism. In his first premiership he seized the opportunity offered by the Dawes Plan and made the most of it, but when he tried a 'Plan' of his own for the benefit of the Russian communists, involving a loan to Russia guaranteed by the British Government, most people felt that his international magnanimity had overstepped the mark, and the other two parties in the House of Commons combined to bring his brief government, which had never enjoyed a Labour party majority, to an end. The unfortunate Labour government of 1929–31, overshadowed almost from the start by the oncoming of the great slump, gave him few opportunities, and when he became prime minister of the National government his powers were already failing. He will live in international history as the principal architect of the London Agreement of 1924 which started the 'period of recovery'.

Baldwin enjoyed a much longer spell of power. What manner of man was this statesman, so greatly admired in his prime and so deeply discredited since his retirement? He was, to begin with, a very fine specimen of a cultured English gentleman. Inheriting a large and prosperous family business, he was also a first cousin of Kipling and a nephew of Burne-Jones. It is difficult to think of him as a ruthless driving force in industry, and indeed he was the author of the remark about the 1919–22 House of Commons, that it was full of 'hard-faced men who looked as though they had done very well out of the war'. He was the least hard-faced of men, generous to a fault; generous in money matters, and generous to his political opponents, whom he never abused after the manner so common among politicians and so tedious to the thoughtful onlooker. His handling of the industrial situation before the general strike was irresolute, but after it had begun and after it was over he displayed a magnanimity worthy of Abraham Lincoln. Indeed, Baldwin's personal character undoubtedly contributed to the result that labour unrest, so conspicuous up to 1926, thereafter rapidly died down. This was widely realized at the time, though it seems since to have been forgotten.[1]

He was not a man of detail and no great pieces of constructive legislation are connected with his name He presided over a team of legislative experts, but did not reckon himself as one of them. He always figured rather as a gifted amateur in politics. His speeches had a distinctive charm and made better reading than those of any other statesman of his day except Churchill. But he was at his best in non-political addresses to non-political audiences—on the Classics, on English Literature, but most of all on the old English countryside, the wholesome and happy ways of a merrier England. He was a nostalgic man.

[1] The view here expressed may be dismissed as a personal idiosyncrasy of my own and when I wrote it I had no authority other than my memory of events twenty years back. But I have since found the same view expressed by Arthur Bryant in 1939. 'In the industrial areas angry strikes paralysed trade and kept nerves taut for years. It was not till the imperceptible but steady hand of Baldwin grasped the tiller in 1923 that the country began once more to feel assured of its own unshakable stability' (*Unfinished Victory*, p. 112.)

In his attitude to foreigners he was very English. He wished his country to stand well with them, but he did not know much about them, and he must have wished that their doings did not require so much attention. He was not altogether fortunate in either of his foreign secretaries, Austen Chamberlain and Sir John Simon. They came in for a great deal of criticism, though their critics had some difficulty in explaining what they ought to have done that they did not do. The rearmament of Germany was the nightmare of his last years in office. He probably could not bring himself to believe that the Germans would be either so wicked or so silly as to provoke the rest of the world to another war, and therein his view coincided with that of the vast majority of his countrymen of all parties right down to the time of his retirement in 1937, and indeed beyond it. It is often said that the National government under MacDonald and Baldwin did nothing for rearmament, but actually it did a good deal, though of course not enough. After he had won the general election of 1935, the last before the war, he made a curious and typically candid admission. He said that he had not proposed to the country as drastic a rearmament programme as the circumstances required, for if he had done so, his government would have been defeated, and the Labour Government that would have replaced it would have done less for rearmament than his government was doing. The statement was devastatingly true, and it annoyed everybody, his supporters and his opponents; probably it dealt his reputation a blow from which it has never recovered. But in so far as he suggested by this admission that there was very little rearmament in his party's election programme he did himself and his party an injustice. There was a lot of rearmament in the programme, as any one can prove who cares to examine the official handbook issued by the party to its candidates for electioneering purposes.

Two other statesmen deserve notice on account of the importance of the parts they played after the period covered by this chapter was over.

Neville Chamberlain lacked Baldwin's personal charm, but he had a harder head. His speeches were rather dull, but he was a first-rate expositor of complicated themes. As Minister of Health in the 1924–9 government and as Chancellor of the Exchequer from the formation of the National government till his appointment as prime minister, he made a reputation as a first-rate administrator. Until he became prime minister he had no first-hand experience of foreign affairs, and this was, no doubt, very unfortunate.

Churchill appears at the beginning of our period as a Liberal coalitionist, like Lloyd George, with whom he had been closely associated ever since they both entered the Liberal Government of 1905. As Secretary of State for War he was responsible for the fruitless efforts to support the anti-Bolshevik forces in Russia. At the election of 1922 he was defeated, and was absent from parliament for two years. At the time of the election of 1924 he was one of a group who planned to displace Baldwin by a reconstruction of the Lloyd George coalition, but the decisive victory of the Conservatives rendered the plan abortive, and he accepted the office of Chancellor of the Exchequer in Baldwin's government, thus returning to the Conservative party which he had left as a very young man in 1903. As chancellor he made finance more interesting than any one had made it since Gladstone's day, and he retained this office throughout the Baldwin government. When the National Government was formed at the height of the great slump he refused to join, partly perhaps because he thoroughly distrusted MacDonald and partly because he disagreed with the policy that the government was about to pursue in India. Thus he was a free lance from 1931 onwards. As a free lance his two chief political activities were opposition to the policy of a further instalment of political responsibility for India, and constantly repeated warnings as to the growing menace from Germany, and the need for a full-scale rearmament. We cannot consider here the relative merits of the Government's India policy and of Churchill's opposition to it, but the coincidence in the time of Churchill's two crusades was doubtless most unfortunate for the credit of the more important of them. In relation to India Churchill appeared as a mere 'die-hard' opponent of the spirit of the age, and those who saw him as such were, most unfortunately, confirmed in their disinclination to take his warnings about Germany as seriously as they deserved to be taken. The India Act passed out of controversy on to the Statute Book in the autumn of 1934, but not until the days of Munich did Churchill entirely regain the confidence either of the House of Commons or the general public.

It is impossible and also unnecessary in a book of this compass, and with the special objective the author has set before himself, to offer a connected narrative of British politics. We have said something of the general strike. The next great event is the great slump, a crisis which the British people confronted and surmounted with the same equanimity. When in the summer of 1931 the Bank of England was known to be in difficulties, an enemy was descried, and we had to gird up our loins and defeat it as we had defeated the Germans. There had to be cuts in expenditure all round, and among the cuts proposed by Snowden, the Labour Chancellor of the Exchequer, supported by his Prime Minister, MacDonald, was a cut in the allowances of the three million unemployed. On this the Labour Government split, a majority of the Cabinet and a large majority of the party refusing to contemplate this unpopular measure. The government resigned, and the King invited MacDonald to form a National government.

When the new government met parliament it was supported by the whole of the Conservative party, the bulk of the Liberal party and a handful of the Labour party. After these measures, together with a budget involving taxation heavier than any of the budgets of the previous war, had been carried, the government appealed to the country, and its policy was endorsed by a majority surpassing even that obtained by Lloyd George in 1918. The Labour party was practically swept out of existence except in the mining constituencies, always the irreducible stronghold of Labour. After the election the government abandoned free trade, a departure to which most Conservatives had looked forward ever since Joseph Chamberlain's tariff reform campaign of 1903. Recovery came slowly. The unemployment figures did not decline perceptibly till 1933, but from the election of 1931 onwards the country was in no doubt that this elusive enemy was doomed. New Year's Day 1932 witnessed the entirely novel spectacle of queues outside the offices of income-tax collectors. Many were reminded of the queues outside recruiting offices in August 1914.

King George V died in January 1936. There was something very instructive about the veneration of his subjects for this admirable man; for he had been a living embodiment of the Victorian virtues, and the feelings with which he was regarded proved that the British people, in spite of the acquisition of so many un-Victorian habits of life and modes of thought, were still largely Victorian at heart. The end of the same year brought the abdication of Edward VIII, a distressing incident which no one could have handled with more tact and dignity than Baldwin. The episode impressed foreign opinion in much the same way as the general strike had done. It illustrated the remarkable quietness and stability of the British people. Many said at the time that the dignity of the British monarchy was irreparably compromised; but it was not so. The incident affected no one but King Edward. He disappeared, and in a few months it was exactly as if he had never been, and George VI had succeeded George V.

In fact, so long as we had only our own affairs to manage, we managed them very well—always excepting the coal industry. But a time was quickly coming when we were not to be left to manage our own affairs.

It was with extreme reluctance that the nation opened its eyes to the prospect of a second German war, and the reluctance of the government reflected all too faithfully in many respects the reluctance of the nation. But its record was not as bad as its retrospective critics, wise after the event, have commonly asserted. The Battle of Britain was won by airmen trained and aircraft constructed under the despised governments of Baldwin and Chamberlain, and since the end of the war we have been furnished with more striking evidence of the activity of these pre-war air ministries.

'How did radar begin? It was late in 1934 that the Air Ministry decided to set up the Committee for the Scientific Survey of Air Defence. One of its officials informally approached a member of the National Physical Laboratory regarding the possibility of a death ray. The reply of the scientists was immediate and definite: there was no early hope of a death ray, but energy reflected from an aircraft could be used to locate it.

'By December 1935 the experimental work was sufficiently far advanced for the Air Ministry to decide on establishing a chain of five radar stations on the east coast of England. This was the first operational radar system installed anywhere in the world. By August 1937 authority was given for fifteen additional stations, giving complete cover to the east and south coasts. In the following year every available experimental equipment was put into operation. The building of a continuous chain of stations from Scotland to the Isle of Wight was accomplished by March 1939, and in order that the warnings of air attack could be flashed from the radar stations to the R.A.F. controllers, and to the civil defence and the public, a new network of

telephone lines thousands of miles in length had to
be specially laid.'[1]

Radar, or radiolocation as it was usually called,
proved to be, first for defence and afterwards for
offence, the most important of all the new scientific
techniques added to the resources of warfare during
the German war of 1939–45, and in the application
of this technique the British Government was, at the
time of the outbreak of the war, far ahead of its
enemy.

THE UNITED STATES

It was by no more than a narrow margin that the
Senate of the United States rejected the Treaty of
Versailles and, with it, American membership of the
League, but their judgment was overwhelmingly
endorsed in the presidential election of 1920. There
seemed nothing to choose between the rival candidates. Harding and Cox were equally insignificant
and their programmes equally nebulous. But Cox
was the Democrat; Wilson was a Democrat; so the
Republican Harding was swept into office on a flood
tide of anti-Wilsonism. He proved not only insignificant but deplorable. His friends were crooks, and he
rewarded them with high office. Three years later
he died, probably by suicide, because revelations
were imminent. One of his chief ministers was
convicted of gigantic frauds and sent to prison.
Others should have followed him. The presidency
passed to Coolidge, an old-fashioned narrow-minded
New Englander whose idea of statesmanship was to
leave things alone. Meanwhile America settled down
to enjoy herself, to grow richer than ever, and to
evade the legislation she had just enacted for the

[1] Article in *The Times*, 15 August 1945.

prohibition of alcoholic drinks. It was the golden age of millionaires, gangsters, and film stars. '*Cette vieille Europe m'ennuie.*' (This old Europe bores me) —the remark attributed to Napoleon summarizes the attitude of inter-war America towards the subjects discussed in this book.

We have already mentioned the American claim to the payment of the war debts due to her from the European belligerents associated with her in the 1914–18 war. Great Britain, as both a creditor and debtor, had suggested that the debts should all be cancelled. This was not the view of President Coolidge, who said, 'They hired the money, didn't they?' The answer to Coolidge is that they did not hire 'money' but goods, and would have been delighted to pay the debt in goods, whatever goods America asked for. Such a repayment would have stimulated British industry, involving as it would have done, the admission of £1,000,000,000 of British goods into America without having to pay the prohibitive American tariff charges; but repayment in goods was made impossible by the American tariffs, now higher than ever. Still, payments were made, somehow or other from 1924 onwards until 1931 when, owing to the great slump, President Hoover proposed a year's respite or moratorium. But when the year was up the American demand was renewed. Some of the debtors, such as France, refused outright. Great Britain, with far the largest liabilities, paid at the end of 1932 her due instalment of £33,000,000 in gold. When the next instalment fell due she offered a 'token payment' of £2,000,000 in silver. Another token payment followed, and then no more. America's rejoinder in 1934 was the

Debt Defaulters Act, depriving the defaulting states of the right to offer any further loans in America to American investors. It is amusing to find an American historian writing, in a book published as recently as 1938: 'One may argue, and with good reason, that this single Act of Congress is accomplishing more to preserve the peace of Europe than the League of Nations. The leading European powers cannot carry on a major war over any considerable period of time without American supplies, and the purchase of such supplies would have to be financed by loans placed in the United States.'[1]

Republican Hoover succeeded Republican Coolidge as President in 1929; he was a millionaire who had made a reputation as an organizer of relief in distressed areas of Europe after the armistice. Before the year was out the inflated bubble of prosperity burst and the slump set in. Hoover and his chief colleagues (also millionaires) had, if their own words are to be believed, entirely failed to foresee the slump. When it came, they said it would soon pass off. When it did not pass off, they entirely failed to deal with it. In November 1932 they were swept out of office in favour of Franklin D. Roosevelt. On the day of Roosevelt's inauguration, in March 1933, every single bank in the United States had closed its doors.

Henceforth Roosevelt, like the National Government in Britain and the National-Socialists in Germany, had to grapple with the problems of the slump. His measures were collectively described as 'A New Deal'. All were courageous; some were

[1] Woodward, W.E., *A New American History*, p. 652.

obvious and some revolutionary; some were successful and some were not; some were intensely unpopular with the wealthy and conservative classes,
and involved Rossevelt in some very hard-hitting
party politics; but he was easily re-elected, on his
domestic anti-slump record, in 1936. But as the
slump slowly retreated before the gallant if somewhat unco-ordinated onslaughts of the New Deal,
America found herself compelled once again to give
her attention to *cette vieille Europe.*

The first great war and their participation in it
had come upon most Americans as a complete
surprise. The second war was foreseen some years
before it arrived and positive measures were taken
to meet the danger it would involve. These measures
were of two kinds. The first, on which America
was practically unanimous, was rearmament. Programmes on an ever-increasing scale were put in
operation very soon after Roosevelt assumed office.
The second was a series of measures designed to
keep America out of the war. On these measures
there was much difference of opinion. In general
terms we may say that the majorities in both
Houses of Congress, while desiring the victory
should fall to the European democracies, put
American pacifism first and the destruction of
Hitlerism a very bad second, whereas Roosevelt and
his Cabinet colleagues reversed the order. They
realized that, if there was a real prospect of a Nazi
conquest of Europe, American pacifism would
have to be abandoned and that, when it came to
the point, the vast majority of Americans would
wish it so.

Insistence on neutral rights of trade with belligerents

had involved America in the first great war. Therefore, said the Isolationist majority in Congress, those rights must be abandoned. In 1935 Congress carried a Neutrality Act prohibiting the export of 'arms, ammunition or any implements of war' to any belligerent nation or any nation which might tranship them to a belligerent. Under this Act America refused to export munitions to Italy for the conquest of Abyssinia, but she did not refuse to export to her materials which were of much more importance to Italy for that purpose, such as oil.

In 1937 Congress passed and Roosevelt reluctantly accepted a second and more stringent Neutrality Act, which maintained all the features of the previous Act and added a 'cash and carry' rule applicable to all American exports. Under this law belligerents could purchase American goods only if they paid for them in cash and carried them away in their own ships. American ships were forbidden to enter belligerent ports. The result of these Neutrality Acts was to penalize, in any war between the dictators and the democracies, the side that the vast majority of Americans wanted to win. In the spring of 1939 Roosevelt pressed for an amendment of these laws, giving the government discretionary powers to suspend their application in an emergency, but the Senate, under the leadership of Senator Borah of Idaho, refused. It is curious and typical that the expression of this refusal should have come from the representative of one of the remotest and obscurest of the Rocky Mountain states, 500 miles from the Pacific and 2,500 from the Atlantic seaboard. Senator Borah told Roosevelt that he had 'his own sources of information', which led him to believe that war was a long way off.

Thus stood American estrangement from Europe when the war began a few months later, but long before the United States entered the war in December 1941 these policies had been reversed and America had become 'the arsenal of democracy'.

IV

THE DOWNWARD SLOPE

THE FAILURE OF THE CONFERENCES

'NEVER', says *The Times* annual summary of 1932, 'was there such a year of international conferences and consultations.' A year passed, and when *The Times* again issued its retrospective supplement it declared that 'the most remarkable developments of the year have been the rise of an aggressive and self-conscious nationalism in Germany and the great economic experiment begun by President Roosevelt in the United States'.

The great slump was an economic collapse on the supernational scale and the most enlightened approach to the problem of economic recovery would obviously be on a scale as wide as the collapse. That meant procedure by international conference, and if international conference were successful it would issue in international collaboration. If the method of international conference failed, then each nation would have to turn to its own economic medicine cupboard, as the only cupboard of which it possessed a key; in other words, each nation would have to seek its own economic salvation by pursuing policies which might of course help but, with equal or greater likelihood, might injure its neighbours.

The first of these conferences met as early as 1930, a Geneva Tariff Conference summoned by the Council of the League at the suggestion of Stresemann, who died before it met. The fatal ideal of national autarky, pursued by means of tariffs, state subsidies, and import quotas, was at any rate one of the factors that had diminished the world's wealth ever since the end of the last war. Could not something be done to break down these hampering regulations and persuade the nations to seek prosperity along lines pursued by an older and wiser generation? Thirty states attended the conference. Most of them brought with them their new projects for higher tariffs, larger subsidies, and stricter quotas as threats for blackmailing their neighbours. The conference failed completely, and in the next year even Great Britain, the last refuge of free trade, found herself compelled to take steps in the direction of autarky.

In November 1931 the German Government announced that a resumption of reparation payments after the conclusion of the 'Hoover moratorium' year would endanger the economic life of the country. Some writers have since said that this was all nonsense and that Brüning's government simply used the slump as an excuse for shuffling out of reparations. It may be so. Certainly any German Government would at any time have seized upon any pretext for shuffling out of reparations. Their incubus was as much psychological as economic. Be that as it may, the Bank of International Settlements, which had been entrusted by the Young Plan with the whole reparations business, upheld Brüning's plea, and recommended an international conference. It met at Lausanne in 1932 and abolished reparations, but failed to rope in America or secure any settlement of the cognate problem of inter-allied debts. These faded out sporadically in the course of the next few years, as has been already recorded, and owing to the manner of their demise forfeited the benefits of an official funeral.

But the main attack upon the slump was to be made by the World Monetary and Economic Conference, which was to seek a substitute for the irrecoverably lost but none the less generally lamented 'gold standard'; in other words, to stabilize the relations between national currencies and provide something like a world-wide money. After many postponements it met in London on 12 June 1933. It was opened by King George V in the Geological Museum at South Kensington, and was attended by the representatives of sixty-six governments—a record among international conferences. After six weeks it adjourned, never to meet again, and with nothing to its credit except an obscure technical agreement about silver. It had in fact been 'torpedoed', as the phrase is, by President Roosevelt. Roosevelt had come into office three months previously and was immersed in the early stages of his 'New Deal'. The dollar had gone off gold and every one seemed much the better for it. He could not allow his hands to be tied by London Conference decisions.

Meanwhile another conference was drawing, after much longer sessions, towards a failure equally complete, the Geneva Disarmament Conference, which met in January 1932, and was adjourned after the defiant withdrawal of Nazi Germany in October 1933.

Disarmament had been on the agenda paper of the civilized world ever since the Treaty of Versailles. The eighth and ninth articles of the Covenant dedicated the League of Nations to this under-taking and declared that a preparatory commission was to be set up. After toying with the subject for some years the Council established the preparatory commission after, and in accordance with the terms of, the Locarno Treaties, and this body, after labours extended over several more years, produced a Draft Scheme which was found to be useless and was almost entirely ignored by the 1932-3 Conference.

Some writers have held that this preoccupation with disarmament as a thing in itself was a mistake, and an example of putting the cart before the horse. Disarmament, they argue, will be a product of security. First achieve security and disarmament will follow; and certainly the notorious absence of security in the inter-war world did in fact render disarmament, outside a few naval agreements, impossible. On the other side it was maintained that the existence of great rival war-machines had been during the period of armed peace before 1914 one of the chief causes of insecurity, that the old Latin tag, *si vis pacem para bellum*, had proved itself the reverse of the truth.

The opening of the conference was most in-auspicious. Japan had just bombarded Shanghai, and the inaugural ceremony had to be adjourned for some hours to enable those members of the conference who were also members of the League Council to consider what was to be done about Japan.

It is unnecessary to enter upon a consideration of the various ingenious and abortive schemes for general disarmament put forward by the representa-tives of the various states. The German delegates brought discussion to the touchstone of reality by demanding equality of status in armaments with the victors of the previous war. Either they must disarm to the German level or Germany must be allowed to rearm, as in fact even before the establishment of Hitler's dictatorship she was already doing. The French delegates blocked this demand and in September 1932 Germany withdrew from the conference. Three months later a Five Power Conference discovered an ambiguous formula which both France and Germany consented to accept, and Germany returned to the conference table. But all the real difficulties remained, and the new year brought with it the consummation of the Nazi dictatorship. In October 1933 Hitler dramatically withdrew Germany from the conference and resigned her membership of the League. Henceforth she would be her own judge in rearmament as in all else. Hitler's decision was enthusiastically endorsed by a plebiscite of the German people, over ninety per cent of whom voted in favour of his policy of defiance.

Less than fifteen years had passed since those dismal figures, Dr. Müller and Dr. Bell, had excited the commiseration of Harold Nicolson as they walked up the Hall of Mirrors to sign the Treaty of Versailles. How and why had Germany passed from the prostration of 1919 to the exaltation of 1933? The previous pages of this book have given, or should have given, the clues required for answering these questions. The course of the 1914–18 war suggested two conclusions, both of them true. The first was that Germany could be, and in fact had been, defeated after immense efforts by a combination f practically all the great powers of the world. The second conclusion was that Germany was one the less far the most powerful nation in Europe, and that nothing short of a renewal of such combination could hold her down. Was the renewal of such a combination at all likely? Nothing in the state of the world in 1933 suggested an affirmative answer to that question. Great Britain, France, Italy, U.S.A., U.S.S.R., Japan—it might be affirmed that not a single one of these major members of the great combination of 1914–18 was on even tolerably friendly terms with any one of the others. For a dozen years Germany had lain prostrate. Now the Nazi magician had summoned her to rise up and walk. There really seemed nothing to prevent her doing so, and she found the change of posture extremely exhilarating.

Even Hitler made one little offering on the altar of disarmament. In the summer of 1935 he offered the British Government an Anglo-German naval treaty in which Germany undertook to keep her total naval tonnage within 35 per cent of that of the British navy. Nothing was said about the numbers of various types of ship. Germany was free, under the treaty, to put the whole of her tonnage into submarines and outbuild us in that department. However, the British Government, delighted to find that Hitler was not as bad as he was painted by his enemies, and realizing that, if the treaty was refused, he would build at least as much as the treaty allowed him, closed with his offer and presented the Anglo-German Naval Treaty to an unadmiring world as a contribution, albeit a little one, to European pacification.

During his final years of retirement, Clemenceau had warned his fellow countrymen against estrangement from Great Britain, begging them always to remember in extenuation of our faults that we were very stupid. He could hardly have found, had he lived long enough, a more apposite illustration of his thesis than this treaty in which, behind the back of France, we give our blessing to a German navy larger than the French one. For Hitler had written a book. 'Would that mine enemy had written a book' said Job in his agony. Our enemy had written one in which he had most obligingly set down all that he was going to do. Never was there such open diplomacy. Hitler was clearly of the school of Bismarck, who said that telling the truth was the diplomatist's trump card, because no one ever believed it. In his book Hitler had said that Germany must make friends with England as a preliminary to smashing France. 'Only with England ... was it possible to begin the new German advance. ... No sacrifice should be too great to win England's favour.'[1] The British negotiators of the Anglo-German naval treaty probably did not remember this passage. The French soon reminded them of it. Hitler had skilfully thrown an apple of discord between the western powers.

ABYSSINIA AND THE RHINELAND

The second chapter of this book gave an outline of international European history down to 1930. The third chapter contained most of the outstanding events between that date and the summer of 1935, but owing to the arrangement of that chapter these

[1] *Mein Kampf* (English edition), p. 154.

ents were scattered about in a number of sketches
national histories so that the pattern of their
ombination in international history was not
pparent. So it will be convenient, before proceed-
g to the history of the last four years of peace, to
recapitulate the events of the two and a half years
ollowing Hitler's accession to power. Most of these
vents have already been mentioned but some have
ot.

In January 1933 Hitler became Chancellor of the
eich, and rapidly transformed his office into a
ctatorship. In October he withdrew from the
isarmament Conference and announced Germany's
tention of rearming. In January 1934 he illus-
ated his pacific intentions by a ten-years' pact of
on-aggression with Poland. Cynics might remark
at Germany had already made, at Locarno, a non-
ggression pact with Poland, not for ten years but
r all futurity. If treaties were worth the paper
ey were written on, why duplicate them? If they
ere not, what purpose did duplication serve?
tatesmen, however, suppressed, for public purposes,
y tendency to cynicism and hoped for the best.

In June 1934 Hitler destroyed the revolutionary
ing of his party, and in July came the murder of
e Austrian chancellor, Dolfuss, by Nazi agents.
pparently an invasion of Austria was intended,
ut Hitler was frightened out of his plans by a firm
rotest of the part of Mussolini. Hitler had to
onsole himself with the fact that the plebiscite of
e inhabitants of the Saar valley, due at this time
nder the terms of the Treaty of Versailles, restored
e province to the Reich by a ninety per cent
ajority of the votes in January 1935.

Meanwhile German rearmament had begun
produce reactions upon her neighbours. In Ju
1934 the British Government announced an a
rearmament programme designed to restore the a
force to the first place among those of Europea
nations. Many readers, indoctrinated by the popula
press with the idea that the MacDonald-Baldwin
Chamberlain Governments did 'nothing' in the wa
of rearmament, at any rate until after the Munic
agreement, will be surprised to find that we entere
on this course so early. No doubt the programm
undertaken was much too small and its pace muc
too leisurely. It was, of course, enormously ou
stripped by the German programme, but it was ne
'nothing'. Indeed, it included radiolocation.

In September 1934 Russia joined the League
Nations which the Soviet Government had hithert
denounced as a capitalist conspiracy and in Ma
1935 Franco-Russian and Franco-Czech treatie
of mutual support against aggression were ratifie
The Russian foreign secretary at this date an
henceforth until shortly before the Russo-German
pact of August 1939 was Litvinov, who had live
for several years in England and had a bette
understanding of and sympathy with the wester
democracies than other Russian statesmen.

In January 1935 Laval, who had succeede
Barthou as foreign minister of France, visited Rom
and negotiated a Franco-Italian treaty. It was
treaty on much the same lines as the Anglo-Frenc
'entente' treaty of 1904. Hitherto, since the end
the last war, France and Italy had been on ba
terms with one another. The treaty sought t
remove points of friction by concessions to Italia

demands in East Africa and in Tunis. It thus would enable France to concentrate on her German frontier troops hitherto pinned down on her Italian frontier. Mussolini valued the treaty as helping to clear the way for his Abyssinian venture.

In March 1935 a visit by the British foreign secretary, Sir John Simon, to Germany for a discussion of German rearmament was arranged. In preparation for the visit the British Government published a White Paper on German rearmament. Hitler thereupon announced that he had a 'cold' and was unable to see Simon. A section of the British press denounced the White Paper as an insult to Germany, and thus encouraged Hitler to proclaim the re-establishment of German conscription. At the same time he announced air force and submarine programmes, both of which were explicitly forbidden by the Treaty of Versailles. Some writers maintain that the real danger period for Hitler was the years 1933–4. Until the end of 1934 his projects could have been nipped in the bud by an invasion which would scarcely have amounted to a war since scarcely any resistance could have been offered. After 1934 suppression of his government would have involved real war, and he rightly gauged that he could go a great deal farther before his neighbours would bring themselves to contemplate that.

The reply to these moves on Hitler's part was the Stresa Conference of April 1935. The British, French, and Italian Governments issued a grave rebuke, which, of course, effected nothing. Mussolini had got himself satisfactorily aligned with the two other Mediterranean powers, for it was they, and not

G

Germany, who could interfere with his Abyssinian project.

Hitler returned a soft answer to the Stresa rebuke in his pacific speech of May 1935. He justified his breaches of the Treaty of Versailles on the ground that that treaty had been a *Diktat* but declared his unswerving loyalty to the Locarno treaties. In particular, he neither wished nor intended to interfere in the internal affairs of Austria. The speech seems to have won commendation from every one of importance except the 'incorrigible war-monger,' Churchill. It is one of the classic examples of Hitler's mendacity. Various writers have compiled long lists of Hitler's broken promises, but we will not follow their example. It can be roundly asserted that there was not a single important action of Hitler's public career which was not a breach, in letter or in spirit, of some previous pledge. But he never lied without a purpose, and his reward of this exhibition of pacifism was the Anglo-German naval treaty of June 1935, which we have already criticized.

Such was the European background of the Abyssinian episode, with which we must now deal. It is a complicated story, and is very easy to denounce the conduct of each of the three great powers involved in it, but much more difficult to arrive at a fair and balanced judgment.

Abyssinia was, with the insignificant exception of Liberia, the only province of Africa not under European control,[1] and the conditions of life there

[1] Except Egypt, but Egypt is not African except in a purely geographical sense. It is, unlike all the rest of Africa, the inheritor of the ruins, spiritual as well as architectural, of ancient civilizations.

prevailing had often been cited by British writers as the strongest argument in favour of the establishment of European rule in that continent. Moreover, a large part of modern Abyssinia consisted of provinces conquered within the previous sixty years by the Amharic Emperors and 'belonged' to Abyssinia only in the same sense as Alsace-Lorraine 'belonged' to Germany after the war of 1870. In the heyday of the 'scramble for Africa' the other great powers had recognized that Abyssinia was to be the prize of Italy, if she could get it, but her efforts had met with inglorious defeat at Adowa in 1896, two years before Kitchener's triumphal conquest of the Sudan. The secret treaty of 1915 which brought Italy into the first great war renewed, by implication, the recognition of Italy's claim. In the postwar years Mussolini pursued a rather curious, and entirely unsuccessful policy of trying to kill Abyssinian independence by kindness. In 1923 he secured Abyssinia's admission to the League of Nations, in face of the opposition of the British Government, which considered the country unfit for that honour, and in 1928 negotiated an Italo-Abyssinian Treaty, in which the parties pledged themselves not to take action detrimental to each other's independence, and to submit all disputes to conciliation and arbitration, without resorting to war. By these singular manœuvres Italy established a cast-iron case against her later policy of direct aggression and conquest which, probably in 1933, Mussolini decided to undertake. A pretext for action was found in a collision between Italian and Abyssinian forces at Walwal, on the frontier of Abyssinia and Italian Somaliland, in January 1935.

This was extremely embarrassing for statesmen outside Italy who had their eyes apprehensively fixed on Germany, and most embarrassing of all for Laval, who had negotiated the Franco-Italian agreement in the same month as the incident at Walwal. The natural reaction of the present-day reader when confronted with the name of Laval is to say to himself 'a traitor, a pro-German', but it is not sensible to suppose that the Laval of 1935 looked forward hopefully to a German conquest of France in order that he might play the ignominious and distressing part of Vichy jackal to the Nazi lions. It would be equally absurd to pretend that Laval was an austere and incorruptible patriot of the type of Poincaré or an international idealist of the type of Briand. He was simply an average French politician of his day (and that is not high praise) trying to do the best for his country. In Laval's view it was all-important to preserve the Franco-Italian entente and the 'Stresa front'. If Mussolini wanted to conquer Abyssinia, what did that matter in comparison? He was breaking several articles of the Covenant of the League? Well, articles of the Covenant had been broken before, by Germany and by Japan. It was very unfortunate, but the purpose of the League was to preserve peace. To take steps which would involve estrangement from, and perhaps war with, Italy over the Abyssinian business would be to sacrifice the end for the sake of the means; and it was unlikely that, if France and Great Britain involved themselves in war with Italy, Germany would be content to look on.

The attitude of the British public was quite different, and Baldwin's government, though beset with anxieties of which the British public took little account, faithfully reflected the outlook of its public. We disapproved of all the dictators, Hitler, Mussolini, and Stalin. We also disapproved of imperialist aggressions, unless they had been our own. We stood for the League and were prepared to make the Abyssinian business a test case of its authority. For the idea of the League had a somewhat stupifying effect upon political thought in our island. It was widely assumed that condemnation by 'the League' would frighten any European country out of any warlike design. It had no doubt failed to frighten Japan, but that was because Japan was so far away. It was not realized that 'the League' was simply the states composing it, and that if those states were inadequately armed or unwilling to employ their arms, the condemnation of 'the League' would be a bluff and its intended victim would probably detect the bluff and snap its fingers at the condemnation. The British Government, on the other hand, realized from the first that a war of 'the League' against Italy would turn out to be a war of Great Britain against Italy. The British public was almost certainly not in favour of an Anglo-Italian war on the Abyssinian question, and in shirking this eventuality Baldwin's government again faithfully interpreted the will of the people, though it got small thanks for its pains.

In March 1935 Abyssinia appealed to the League on the Walwal incident. The Council kept the embarrassing problem in cold storage as long as possible but at its meeting in September, when an Italian invasion of Abyssinia was obviously imminent, Sir Samuel Hoare delivered a powerful speech in favour of 'the collective maintenance of the Covenant in its entirety and particularly for the steady and collective resistance to all acts of unprovoked aggression'. All small states threatened by powerful neighbours were delighted. Laval was seriously alarmed, but determined to avoid a break with Britain. In October Italy invaded Abyssinia and a very large majority of members of the League proceeded to impose 'sanctions' on Italy under Article 16 of the Covenant. The members voting for 'sanctions' undertook to stop exportation to Italy of various implements of war. None of them were implements of which Italy stood in urgent need, and the prohibitions were not to take effect until 18 November. This fell a very long way short of Article 16 under which *all* members of the League should have undertaken *immediately* to subject the delinquent state to the severance of *all* trade relations. In particular no sanction was imposed upon oil, and it was notorious that an oil embargo was the one measure short of war, or the closing of the Suez Canal, which might have brought the Italian invasion to a standstill. Mussolini accepted these moral rebukes and innocuous sanctions with exemplary meekness, and went ahead with his invasion, though the military results of the first two months' hostilities were not very impressive. The British Government strengthened its Mediterranean fleet and its garrisons in Malta, Egypt, and Aden. No other member of the League took any military measures whatever.

Meanwhile the British Government dissolved parliament and the last general election before the second great war was held. The government were blamed for holding the election at this time, and it certainly worked out to their advantage, but four years had passed since the previous election and the event could not have been long postponed. The Abyssinian question thrust all other issues into the background, and the opposition parties could find very little fault with the policy of the government which consequently secured a far larger majority than it would have done six months earlier or six months later.

In December Laval persuaded Hoare to meet him in Paris. Laval felt that the game of sanctions had gone far enough. If, as was being suggested, further sanctions were to be imposed Italy must first be given an opportunity of accepting or rejecting a compromise solution of the Abyssinian problem. The result was the Hoare-Laval proposal offering Italy about half the country, namely the lowlying areas to the east and south of the highlands which constituted the home of the Amharic race. The publication of the proposals roused an instant and universal storm of abuse in Great Britain. Hoare resigned and the government repudiated the scheme to which he had given his name.

The rejection of the Hoare-Laval proposal was a striking illustration of the potency of British democracy. Here was a government recently returned to power with an enormous majority on the strength of a 'sanctions' policy. A month later it was seen to be turning aside from its resolve. An immediate outburst of public opinion compelled it to retrace its steps. The Labour opposition was fully entitled to say that, if the Hoare-Laval proposal had preceded the election the government would have got a much smaller majority or none at all, but it was wide of the mark when it asserted that the whole thing was a deep-laid plot and that the Conservatives had cried 'sanctions' in their election campaign with their tongues in their cheeks. Stanley Baldwin was no Machiavelli; perhaps he was not Machiavellian enough.

As for Laval, the British rejection of the Hoare-Laval proposals led to the fall of his government, and it may be that from this date onwards he cherished a grievance against Britain which led to his becoming a Vichyite in 1940.

Mussolini went ahead and completed the conquest of Abyssinia in the ensuing spring. It was an ugly story, but not much more ugly than the British conquest of Rhodesia forty years before, the main difference being that aircraft and mustard gas were unknown in the days of Rhodes and Jameson.[1] Thenceforth Mussolini linked the fortunes of Italy with those of Germany.

It is easy to be wise after the event and to see that the policy pursued by the British Government was illogical and disastrous. One could make a case in favour of going all out for the principles of the League against Italy and facing a war in which Great Britain would have been to all intents and purposes, the sole champion of the Covenant. We shirked it, not because we were afraid of a naval war with Italy but because we felt certain that such a war would open up another general war. Short of such a policy as this, the only sound alternative

---

[1] But the Matabele War, or conquest of Rhodesia, was also facilitated by a new weapon, denounced at the time as diabolical, namely the machine-gun.

was to sacrifice Abyssinia in order to preserve the Stresa front against Germany, much as Sir Edward Grey sacrificed Persia in order to preserve the Anglo-Russian entente against Germany in 1911. But this would not have been tolerated by British public opinion. So we pursued an 'unhappy mean' of sham sanctions which involved the break-up of the Stresa front without rendering any service to Abyssinia.

The sanctions fiasco did not prove the end of European peace but it marked, for all practical purposes, the end of the League. In the later crises, the Munich crisis for example, the League neither helped nor hindered; it was not there. International relations in the last years before the second great war had reverted to the technique of the years preceding the first great war.

Britain had irritated France by the Anglo-German naval treaty: France had irritated Britain by the Hoare-Laval proposals which, it was supposed, a crafty French politician had imposed upon a weak-minded British foreign secretary: both had alienated Italy by the sanctions policy. Moreover, a French general election was due in the spring of 1936 and it was likely to be contested on domestic issues with exceptional bitterness. The time was ripe, from Hitler's standpoint, for an all-important and hazardous forward move. On 7 March the signatory states of the Treaty of Locarno were informed that German troops were marching into the demilitarized Rhineland. A week earlier he had given an interview to a journalist in which he declared that the idea of war between France and Germany was an absurdity, and expressly repudiated the passages in *Mein Kampf* referring to the necessity of destroying France, alleging in extenuation of them that they were written at the time of the occupation of the Ruhr—which they were not; they were written at the time of the Locarno Conference. Immediately after the occupation of the Rhineland he offered a new non-aggression treaty to the states whose previous treaty with Germany he had just torn up. It seems absurd to-day that such an offer should have been treated with anything but contempt, but it was welcomed by *The Times*, though not by the new foreign secretary, Anthony Eden.

The occupation of the Rhineland, like so many other actions of Nazi Germany in these years posed the dilemma expressed by Burke when he wrote: 'It is no inconsiderable part of wisdom to know how much of an evil ought to be tolerated.' Poland and Czechoslovakia declared their readiness to mobilize if Great Britain and France would intervene; but France was afraid and Britain unwilling. To France the remilitarization of the Rhineland was a far worse offence than the conquest of Abyssinia. The latter was merely a concluding act of the 'scramble for Africa' in which half a dozen countries had taken shares; the former was the destruction of the principal security against invasion granted to France and Belgium by the Treaty of Versailles. To the British public, on the other hand, the remilitarization of the Rhineland was one of those things that was bound to happen sooner or later. It was not in the nature of things that a sovereign state should consent for an indefinite period to leave part of its own territory unfortified and exposed to invasion.

The Rhineland provisions of the Treaty of Versailles seemed to be of the same order that Black Sea clauses of the treaty following the Crimean War, forbidding Russia to have a naval base on that sea. When Palmerston was asked how long he thought those arrangements would last, he answered 'they will last my time'—and he was then seventy-one!

Those who criticize the failure of Baldwin's government to keep Hitler out of the Rhineland, should consider the only alternative policy, namely war; and a little consideration will show that war was impossible, not because Germany could not at that stage have been defeated—she could have been defeated more easily than in 1939—but because the British people would not have stood it. The British people will stand a European war only when provoked by a flagrant act of wickedness—usually an act of the kind described in schoolboy language as bullying. The remilitarization of the Rhineland might, indeed certainly did, facilitate future acts of bullying, but it was not in itself an act of bullying, and until King Demos has become much more of a philosopher king than he is at present, democratic governments cannot, on issues of life and death, take long views, when the obvious emotional reactions of the people point in another direction.

SPAIN, AUSTRIA, CZECHOSLOVAKIA, POLAND

The Abyssinian episode had alienated Italy from Britain and France and consequently pushed her in the direction of Germany. The chief bone of contention between the two dictators was Austria, for a German occupation of Austria would bring the frontier of Germany right up to the Brenner Pass, beyond which a German minority was suffering from Italian rule. It only needed a further packet of lies from Hitler to eliminate this 'bone', and lull to sleep suspicions which Mussolini was perhaps not very anxious to keep awake; for he took a personal pride in the achievements of his German pupil. Some time in the early summer of 1936 Mussolini was given a private view of a new Austro-German treaty, published in July, which recognized the 'full sovereignty' of Austria, each party to the treaty, the wolf and the lamb, pledging itself to refrain from interfering in the 'internal affairs' of the other. If this meant anything (which of course it did not) it meant that the lamb was no longer in danger of becoming part of the internal affairs of the wolf. In November the 'Berlin-Rome Axis' was proclaimed.

Meanwhile, in July, civil war had broken out in Spain. Spain, even more obviously than France, had never recovered equilibrium after her experiences in the French revolutionary epoch. The expulsion of Napoleon's armies from Spain had meant both a restoration of a very old-fashioned despotic monarchy and a triumph of nineteenth-century Liberalism. Indeed it was in Spain that the word 'liberal' was first introduced into political currency. The Spaniards, with their fierce uncompromising character and an illiteracy which even in 1931 embraced almost half the population, are singularly ill-fitted for parliamentary democracy, and parliamentary government in Spain has constantly been punctuated by *coups* carried out by military dictators. The civil war of 1936–9 merely reproduced, with modern modifications, the Carlist wars of a hundred years earlier, and involved for Europe in general the same problems of intervention or non-intervention.

The more recent history of Spain must be briefly summarized. In 1923 Primo de Rivera had established a dictatorship, but the Liberals had secured his resignation in 1930, and in 1931 the abolition of the monarchy. The republican constitution then established proved a failure from the start, if the test of success is the maintenance of order. In 1932 there was a revolt of the royalists; in 1933 a revolt of the Anarcho-Syndicalists, who may be regarded as a Spanish variety of Communist, in that they stood for a dictatorship of the Left. The elections of 1933 gave a majority to the Conservative parties. In the election of February 1936 the opposing forces were almost equally balanced, the Conservatives having a small majority among the voters, but the chances of the poll gave a small majority of seats to a 'Popular Front', which included everything from Liberals who believed in parliamentary government to Anarcho-Syndicalists who emphatically did not. These latter took the law into their own hands, and in the five months between the elections and the outbreak of the civil war destroyed 251 churches and 324 opposition newspaper offices. These were the 'Liberals' with whom the western democracies were invited to sympathize by their own Left-wing parties.

Franco's rebellion was intended to be a *coup d'état* of the short and sharp variety familiar in Spanish history. In this respect it failed, and its victory was achieved only after nearly three years of ferocious civil war. As soon as it became apparent that the struggle would be prolonged the British and French governments issued an appeal to all other European governments inviting them to pledge themselves to a policy of non-intervention in Spanish affairs. All of them assented, and an international non-intervention committee was established in London in September 1936. But the actions of certain governments failed to correspond with their professions. Italy had certainly been privy to Franco's revolt and had supported it from the start, and German assistance soon followed. Without assistance from Italy Franco's rebellion would probably have fizzled out like the royalist rebellion of 1932. On the other side, as soon as it became plain that 'the Government', or the Liberals, or the Syndicalists (whatever one pleases to call them) were making a good fight of it, Russian assistance began to flow into the Mediterranean ports held by this party, thereby prolonging for over two years a resistance which would otherwise have collapsed in a few months. Small numbers of misguided enthusiasts from Britain and France and elsewhere joined in the fray on one side or the other. Non-intervention became a farce. Few committees have ever listened to as many lies as the London non-intervention committee.

It was commonly said that the interventions of Italy, Germany, and Russia in the Spanish civil war were dictated by ideological motives, the Fascist states supporting Spanish Fascism and Communist Russia supporting Spanish Communism much as Catholic and Protestant monarchies had supported Catholic and Protestant parties in other countries in the sixteenth century. But students of the sixteenth century know very well that Catholic and Protestant monarchs never supported rebels of their own creed elsewhere unless they had some purely political motive for doing so. Where the political motive was lacking identity of religion counted for little or nothing. It is notorious, for example, that Catholic France pursued for long periods what is absurdly called a 'Protestant foreign policy', supporting Protestant rebels in Germany at the very same time as she was suppressing her own Protestant rebels at home. One must therefore ask what purely political, or national, motives lay behind the apparently ideological activities of the intervening powers, and it is then seen that they were manœuvring for favourable positions in the event of the outbreak of another European war. In seeking to establish a protégé dictator in Spain Hitler was copying with curious exactness the policy of Bismarck when he sought, by means of the less barbarous but equally immoral techniques of his day, to establish a protégé Hohenzollern on the Spanish throne. In each case France would be encircled, and her military concentration against her main enemy would be distracted by the possibility of a stab in the back from the protégé. From Italy's point of view a friendly Spain might embarrass or even render impossible British naval power in the Mediterranean. The Russian motive is less obvious except in so far as every German motive for supporting Franco was automatically a Russian reason for opposing him.

Judged by results one may say that all the interveners miscalculated the future and wasted their energies. Though naturally and undisguisedly

sympathetic to the Axis powers Franco observed a
fairly correct neutrality throughout the second great
war. It is true that he sent a Spanish division to
fight under German orders against Russia, but very
likely the service he thus rendered to the Germans
was less than the service he rendered their enemies
by turning a blind eye to various technical breaches
of neutrality committed by the Anglo-American
naval concentrations at Gibraltar previous to the
invasion of North Africa in 1942. It is of course true
that Spain sold to Germany during the war a great
deal of valuable material, but she would have done
the same under a government of any political
complexion. Neutrals almost always make all the
money they can out of selling materials to any
belligerent in a position to buy them. It looks as if
the war of 1939–45 was entirely unaffected by the
outcome of the Spanish civil war of 1936–9. That
being so the fuss about the Spanish civil war was,
for every one but the Spaniards themselves, a fuss
about nothing.[1]

It was Hitler's custom to deliver a speech covering
a general survey of affairs on each 30 January, the
anniversary of his acceptance of the chancellorship.
In the speech delivered on that occasion in 1937 he

---

[1] We have heard since the end of the war that Franco offered
to join the Axis powers in 1941 if they would help him to
recover Gibraltar, and *The New Statesman* (5 July 1945),
asks us to regard this as an additional reason for his condemnation by the victorious allies. But if Great Britain had lost, say,
the Isle of Wight to a predominant naval power two hundred
years ago, any British government to-day would probably
ally itself with any belligerent that would help her to get it
back. If Germany and Italy had been in a position to capture
Gibraltar they would have captured it without any
invitation from Franco.

declared that 'the period of so-called surprises is at
an end', and the statement remained true for the
remainder of the year, the most important development apart from the progress of the Spanish civil
war being another purge in the upper regions of the
Nazi hierarchy. It was a quiet affair compared with
the purge of 1934, the process being resignation
instead of murder, and the victims being of the
Right instead of the Left and a mere handful in
numbers, but in the upshot it proved equally
important. Fourteen highly placed military officers
of Conservative and cautious views were removed
from their commands, and the parvenu adventurer
Ribbentrop succeeded the more moderate Neurath
as foreign minister. On 30 January 1938 Hitler
postponed his annual oration for three weeks as
though he were not quite ready for it, and before
the three weeks were completed Schuschnigg,
the Austrian chancellor, had been summoned to
Hitler's country house at Berchtesgaden and compelled to accept the Nazi Seyss-Inquart, who
was not an Austrian at all, as his Minister for the
Interior.

This was plainly a tearing up of the Austro-
German treaty of 1936 which had brought Italy
into the Axis, and Chamberlain, true to his policy
of conciliation, sought to lure Italy back to her
Stresa policy by an Anglo-Italian pact in which
bygones would be accepted as bygones, the Italian
conquest of Abyssinia recognized and the Italian
intervention in Spain condoned, provided that
Italian troops were now withdrawn. The inception
of this policy led to the resignation of his foreign
secretary, Anthony Eden, who was succeeded by

Lord Halifax. Eden held that the attempt to conciliate Italy would be an exhibition of weakness which would do more harm than good. Chamberlain held that Italy's real interests lay in the direction of co-operation with the western democracies and that Mussolini, if kindly treated, would have the sense to realize the fact. He was right on the first point and wrong on the second, as subsequent events were to show. An Anglo-Italian agreement was ultimately concluded, on paper, but it was not worth the paper on which it was written, for Mussolini never made any pretence of observing its terms.

Months before the conclusion of the Anglo-Italian agreement, however, Austria had ceased to exist. Encouraged by the appointment of Seyss-Inquart the Austrian Nazis became more and more disorderly. On 9 March Schuschnigg announced the holding of a plebiscite on the following Sunday, in which the whole people would be asked to vote for or against the continuance of Austrian independence. It was expected that he would secure a two-thirds or three-quarters majority, and Hitler determined to intervene at once. He demanded the postponement of the plebiscite and, when this was granted, further demanded the resignation of Schuschnigg and the allocation of two-thirds of the seats in the Cabinet to Nazis. Meanwhile, German forces, provided with detailed instructions, which had evidently been prepared before the plebiscite crisis opened, invaded the country. By Schuschnigg's orders there was no resistance, and in twenty-four hours Austria had become a province of the Reich.

By annexing Austria, whose independence Mussolini had stoutly and effectively championed four years before, at the time of the murder of Dollfuss, Hitler subjected the Axis to a strain. It proved, however, strong enough to bear it. The Duce did not raise a finger on behalf of his former ally and was rewarded with fulsome compliments from the Führer—and with the rather curious assurance that Italy's frontiers would be henceforth as safe as those of France. This sounds like a joke; probably the idea was to give France an oblique assurance that her frontiers were as secure as those of Italy.

The 'rape of Austria' was for Germany's Danubian ambitions what the remilitarization of the Rhineland had been for her westward ambitions. It established her in a commanding position for a further offensive. As Churchill said in the House of Commons, 'Mastery of Vienna gives to Nazi Germany military and economic control of the whole of the communications of south-eastern Europe, by road, by river, and by rail'. It also enormously increased her supplies of iron and timber. In this case as in the Rhineland, Hitler had chosen a line of aggression against which it was impossible for the western democracies to make a protest such as would enlist that unanimous and enthusiastic support without which war cannot be effectively undertaken. Those who wanted to make the best of a bad job reminded themselves that the Austrians were, after all, Germans, and that the prohibition of the *Anschluss*, or union of Germany and Austria, after the last war, had been widely condemned by authorities supposed to be liberal and enlightened.

The fall of Austria obviously placed Czechoslovakia in extreme jeopardy. A glance at the new map presenting Austria as a province of the Reich showed Czechoslovakia as a sort of cigar with half of it, the thicker end, inside a grim German mouth, the newly annexed Austria constituting the lower jaw. In other words, Bohemia, the Czech province of the republic, was surrounded on three sides, north, west, and south by German territory.

In dealing with the Rhineland and with Austria Hitler had achieved his aim by a single stroke. In dealing with Czechoslovakia no great degree of artfulness was needed to suggest that he had better take two bites at the cherry, declaring as he took the first bite that the second one was quite unthinkable. It was a fortunate circumstance from his point of view that a wide strip of Bohemia all round its German frontiers was predominantly inhabited by people of German race, the so-called Sudeten Germans, 3,200,000 in number, nearly a quarter of the whole population of the country. British statesmanship still professed allegiance to the principle of nationalistic self-determination. It would be almost as difficult for a British government to make a *casus belli* of a German claim to the land of the Sudeten Germans as of a German claim to the land of the Austrian Germans, if the Sudeten Germans were sufficiently stimulated to agitate for union with their fellow nationals. There would remain an indefensible 'rump' of Czech and Slovak Czechoslovakia; this could have its integrity solemnly guaranteed— and be dealt with another day. No doubt, in Hitler's opinion, British statesmen, and the French statesmen who now followed meekly in their wake, were very great fools to draw these old-fashioned distinctions between what was right and wrong in the matter of annexations. No doubt they would be even more foolish to swallow with satisfaction any more Hitlerite promises. His business was to play up to their folly, leaving its exposure to some future occasion. Actually their folly, though great, was less abysmal than that of Hitler in his infatuated belief that he could go on playing that game for ever. The road was to be long and terrible for all concerned, but Hitler was already on the road to the suicide scene in the Berlin air-raid shelter of May 1945.

Within a few weeks of the annexation of Austria the German press and wireless opened a campaign denouncing the atrocities committed by the Czech authorities against the poor oppressed Sudetens, a propaganda which was surely an insult to human intelligence. Could any one suppose that the Czechs who, on the negative evidence of the absence of German protests, had behaved perfectly correctly to the Sudetens during the preceding years, had suddenly transformed themselves into fiends at the very moment when their country became the next German objective.[1] Henlein, hitherto the local leader of the Sudetens, became Hitler's agent, and it was from a German city that in April he published a formal demand for complete autonomy for all areas in which the Sudetens constituted a majority of the population. This would mean in effect the

[1] Sudeten villages were ordered by the German Government to select one of their number and send him or her to Berlin as a specimen victim of Czech outrage. An Englishman encountered one of these persons, a woman, in Berlin during the summer of 1938. She laboured under a grievance because she had been promised that she would be allowed to return home in a fortnight, and that interval of time had been long exceeded. See *Germany between the Wars*, by Lindley Fraser, p. 139.

separation from Czechoslovakia of a strip of territory varying in width from ten miles to fifty miles all round the north, west and south of Bohemia, involving the abandonment of the fortified mountain frontier and of the important Skoda munition works. It was obvious that the 'autonomy' of this area would be simply a euphemism for its absorption in the Reich.

France and Russia were both bound by recent treaties to defend the integrity of Czechoslovak territory. Great Britain was under no such written obligation apart from her general obligations under the Covenant of the League, but she was bound to France by the Treaty of Locarno and it was well understood that Britain would not remain neutral in a Franco-German war. In these circumstances the British Government sent Lord Runciman, an ex-Cabinet minister, to Prague to assist the Czechs in their efforts to bridge the gap between what Henlein demanded and what they were prepared to grant. Such efforts were, of course, predestined to failure. President Beneš was in the same position as Schuschnigg had been in a very few months before. Hitler did not intend a settlement within the frontiers of Czechoslovakia. He intended to bite off the first half of the cherry. The only question at issue was whether his action would involve a general war.

War seemed inevitable when, on 15 September, Chamberlain arranged a personal meeting with Hitler and, entering an aeroplane for the first time in his life, flew to Berchtesgaden. The warm welcome he received from German crowds on his arrival at the aerodrome showed that the German people were as anxious to avoid war as he was himself.[1] Hitler demanded the immediate incorporation in the Reich of all areas containing an over 50 per cent German population.[1] Chamberlain returned with the demand, secured the agreement of the French Government and the assent, under strong protest, of the Czech Government. While he was thus occupied, Poland and Hungary, playing jackal to the German lion, put in claims to the districts of Slovakia in which their nationals predominated, and Hitler exhibited his disinterestedness by taking their claims under his patronage.

Having secured French and Czech assent to the Berchtesgaden ultimatum, Chamberlain again flew to Germany on 23 September, this time meeting Hitler at Godesberg in the Rhineland. Geographically Hitler had come half-way to meet him, but in other respects he had moved in the opposite direction. Closely copying his Austrian technique of a second ultimatum close on the heels of the acceptance of the first, he stiffened his demands in a variety of particulars, demanding for example that the Sudeten territory should be handed over with all its fortifications and commercial installations, railway rolling stock, foodstuffs, cattle and raw materials intact. These terms were rejected by the Czechs and denounced by Chamberlain in the course of a stormy interview with the Führer. He returned to England

---

[1] The wits invented various fragments of conversation between Hitler and Chamberlain at the Berchtesgaden interview, among them the following:

H. You must remember, Mr. Chamberlain, that if war comes again we shall have the Italians on our side this time.

C. Well, that seems only fair; we had to have them last time.

and ordered immediate mobilization. Thereupon Mussolini, either of his own accord or by arrangement with Hitler, proposed a four-power conference at Munich on 29 September. The Munich Agreement 'saved the face' of the British and French Governments by modifying in certain unimportant details the Godesberg ultimatum. It was not accepted by the Czech Government, which thus went down with its flag flying reproachfully to its allies and defiantly to its enemies. The Agreement also contained a clause renouncing resort to war in the settlement of Anglo-German differences.

Chamberlain is not to be overmuch blamed for the fact that on arrival in England, surrounded by cheering crowds, he let slip the fatuously optimistic remark that he brought back with him 'peace in our time'. What was more important was that he immediately ordered the redoubling of the rearmament programme.

The Munich Agreement was the last and, in the judgment of critics, the worst example of the 'policy of appeasement' associated with Chamberlain's name. That policy was so completely discredited by subsequent events that it is necessary for the historian to present it as it appeared at the time. There is no doubt at all that it was accepted by the overwhelming majority of the British people of all classes and all parties. Its critics were remarkable for their weight and eminence but not for their numbers. Foremost among them, of course, was Churchill, and with him were Eden, Duff Cooper, Lord Cranborne, and Harold Nicolson. On the special issue of Czechoslovakia Hitler had once again chosen a good case, a case in which British opinion saw arguments on both sides. There was the Irish analogy. The Irish Free State was, no doubt, like Czechoslovakia, entitled to govern itself, but it was not entitled to govern Northern Ireland so long as Northern Ireland preferred London to Dublin. Sudetenland could plausibly be regarded as the Northern Ireland of Czechoslovakia.

On the more general issue Chamberlain was true to the best British traditions in holding that war should be avoided on all issues on which a reasonable, even though not an ideal, solution could be secured without it. Where he was entirely wrong was in his diagnosis of Hitler's ambitions. He held that Hitler had certain limited aims, roughly speaking the incorporation within the Reich of all territories bordering on Germany which were mainly inhabited by Germans. If a peaceful arrangement of these successive aims could be secured, then, when they were all satisfied—and the number of such claims was strictly limited—a troubled world might reasonably look forward to quieter times. On this point he was entirely wrong, and his critics were entirely right. The appeasement policy was based on a false diagnosis, and it is easy to be wise after the event, but it was not a policy of weakness. It would be absurd, for example, to suggest that Chamberlain led the country into war over Poland in 1939 and refrained from leading the country into war over Czechoslovakia in 1938 because by 1939 we were better armed. No doubt we were better armed in 1939, but so also was Germany. In 1938 we would have had the probable support of Russia—so we are told—whereas in 1939 we entered the war immediately after learning that Russia had made a pact with the enemy. The difference between 1939 and 1938 was that by 1939 the Chamberlain diagnosis of Hitler's ambitions had been proved wrong, six months earlier, by the annexation of the non-German remainder of Czechoslovakia.

Thousands of people far inferior to Neville Chamberlain in intelligence and courage, people who applauded him for saving them from war in 1938, have since his resignation and death lost no opportunity of pouring scorn on his name. One man, his equal in courage and his superior in intelligence, a man who consistently denounced the appeasement policy both after Munich and long before it, has never poured scorn on his name. Winston Churchill took office under Chamberlain when the war began, spoke in his defence in the debate eight months later which led to Chamberlain's resignation, and offered him a seat in his own War Cabinet. Speaking in November 1939 Churchill said of Chamberlain: 'He is a man of very tough fibre, and I can tell you that he is going to fight as obstinately for victory as he did for peace.'

We may grant, then, that the appeasement policy was obstinately wrong-headed, and yet we may be glad that it was pursued to the uttermost. We did not, in the upshot, sacrifice a Czechoslovakia we could otherwise have rescued, for if war had broken out in 1938 Czechoslovakia would as surely have been occupied by the enemy for the duration of the war as Poland was in 1939. But by pursuing the policy of appeasement up to the very last minute of the time during which German demands kept within limits for which a shadow of justification could be offered, we proved up to the hilt that the war, when it came, was entirely justified and absolutely inevitable.

There was one other ground on which the policy of appeasement might be, and sometimes has been, condemned. It is said that we were morally in the wrong in remaining at peace with Nazi Germany, because of the abominable way in which the Nazi Government behaved towards a minority of their own subjects, more particularly their Jews. It is natural that this line of argument should have been pursued with some vehemence by Jewish publicists outside Germany. It is the line of argument by which Gladstone advocated a European 'crusade' against Turkey on account of the Armenian massacres in the 1890's, and Churchill came near advocating a crusade against 'the foul baboonery' of Bolshevism after the end of the first great war. But it is doubtful if a nation ever has provoked, or ever ought to provoke, a first-class war in order to chastise its neighbours for their domestic misdeeds. There is here no clear general principle. It is a question of measuring the magnitude of the evil involved in the remedy against the evil to be remedied. It was right, we may hold, to send a small punitive expedition in 1897 to stamp out the horrors of human sacrifice in the Nigerian Sultanate of Benin, simply because the thing could be easily and cheaply done. Belsen[1] was as bad as Benin—nay, much worse: but it was very much more difficult to get at. We are brought back again to Burke's dictum: 'It is no inconsiderable part of statesmanship to know how much of an evil ought to be tolerated.'

[1] One of the German torture camps exposed by Allied occupation in 1945.

The months immediately following Munich were quiet in comparison with the previous summer, for as Goebbels explained, 'the boa-constrictor needed to digest all that it had eaten before it started again'. In Germany the persecution of the Jews was intensified. In Italy an allusion by the foreign minister, Ciano, to 'the natural aspirations of the Italian people' was greeted with shouts of 'Tunis! Nice! Corsica!' and it was generally assumed that these interruptions had been arranged in advance by agents of the government.[1] Franco's troops captured Barcelona, the headquarters of the republicans or syndicalists in January 1939, and thereafter the Spanish civil war drew rapidly to its close. Hitler's annual speech on 30 January emphasized the value of the German-Polish treaty of 1934 and eulogized the late Polish dictator, Pilsudski. Hope sprang eternal once more in the British breast, and Sir Samuel Hoare denounced alarmists as 'jitterbugs'. Then, in the middle of March, came the final destruction of Czechoslovakia. It is unnecessary to go into the details of the transaction, except to say that Hitler once again cast himself for the part of the deliverer of an oppressed people. Trouble was fomented between the Czechs and the Slovaks, and Father Tiso, the Slovak premier (for Czechoslovakia had been converted into a federal state of three provinces, Bohemia, Slovakia, and Ruthenia, after the Munich settlement) was induced to play the part

[1] Tunis had been occupied by France in 1880, at which date it already contained some thousands of Italian settlers. Nice had been ceded to France by Italy in return for the help given by Napoleon III in the *Risorgimento* campaign of 1859. Corsica had been occupied by France in 1768, being at that time in revolt against the rule of the Republic of Genoa.

previously enacted by Henlein. Bohemia and Slovakia were added to the Reich on the ground that they had always been part of the German *Lebensraum* (living space), and Ruthenia was thrown to Hungary.

With this event the whole philosophy of appeasement crashed to the ground. Hitler had at last annexed a territory which was not inhabited by Germans. The British Government entered at once on a course of policy which it had refused at Locarno and ever since. It proceeded to negotiate treaties of alliance with all the states in eastern Europe which might be attacked by Germany—Poland, Rumania, and Greece.

The Greek treaty was a consequence of Mussolini's Good Friday onslaught upon Albania. Regarded as a thing in itself, this was of small importance. Mussolini obviously wanted to demonstrate to his countrymen that there was more than one dictator in Europe capable of committing 'rapes' on inoffensive neighbours. But in so far as Italy was to be regarded as Germany's ally it was evidence that the Axis had inserted a wedge into the Balkan peninsula, which could be widened in any direction at the expense of any of the Balkan states.

But it was already plain that the next item on the programme was Poland. Here the place of the Sudeten grievance was taken by Danzig and the Polish corridor. Danzig, on the western frontier of the isolated German province of East Prussia, was unquestionably a German city, one of the Hansa towns of the Middle Ages, but at the same time it was the natural sea-outlet of Polish trade. The Treaty of Versailles had sought to do justice to both aspects of the situation by making Danzig a free city governed by its inhabitants and entrusting to Poland the control of its harbour. A neutral commissioner appointed by the League had the duty of securing fair play between the rival authorities. It was from the first a thankless task, and a wellnigh impossible one after the municipal government of Danzig had been captured by the local Nazis. One of the grievances of the Danzigers was that Poland had created a new and rival port farther down the estuary of the Vistula on her own soil at Gdynia. The term 'Polish corridor' suggested that this strip of territory isolating Danzig on the west from the main body of the Reich had been given to Poland as an outlet to the sea. Actually it was given to her because its inhabitants were predominantly Polish. It was part of the province of Pomorze, or West Prussia, which had belonged to Poland for hundreds of years previous to its seizure by Frederick the Great in 1772. In fact the isolation of East Prussia from the rest of the territories ruled from Berlin, whatever the case against it, had been an accepted fact of political geography from 1619, when the Elector of Brandenburg acquired East Prussia by a genealogical accident, down to 1772.

In March 1939 Germany proposed that, subject to retention by Poland of her commercial rights in the harbour, Danzig should be absorbed into the Reich; also that Germany should be granted full control of an east and west road and rail route across the corridor. Poland rejected these terms, and immediately afterwards the British Government negotiated the treaty of alliance with Poland already mentioned. Thereupon Hitler denounced both the German-Polish treaty of 1934 and the Anglo-German naval agreement of 1935. At the same time the German press began to advertise Polish atrocities against German subjects similar to the alleged Czech atrocities denounced in the previous year.

The course was now set for another crisis, and the details of the various manœuvres between Poland and Germany are of little interest. The world's attention was abruptly focused on Russia, who had been, unwisely perhaps, excluded from the negotiations over Czechoslovakia on the ground that the inclusion of 'the Bolshevists' would only further exacerbate the temper of the Nazis. British negotiations were opened with Russia in April and at once received a serious setback when Litvinov, the foreign secretary friendly to the western democracies, was dismissed and succeeded by Molotov. Russia in fact intended to secure her eastern frontier against Germany by annexing the small Baltic republics of Estonia, Latvia, and Lithuania, which had been lost to her after the first great war, by pushing back the frontier of Finland, which was only fifteen miles from Leningrad, and by securing for herself the extensive provinces, mainly inhabited by Russians, which had been occupied by Poland, in defiance of the 1919 peace settlement, after her victory over Russia on the Vistula in 1920. Along these lines Great Britain was not prepared to negotiate. The Germans, of course, had no such scruples. Just as Poland, the victim of 1939, had readily shared with Germany the carcass of Czechoslovakia in 1938, so Russia, who was to be the victim of 1941, agreed to share with Germany the carcass of Poland in 1939. Stalin carried 'appeasement' a great deal farther than Chamberlain. The Russo-German pact was announced on 23 August. Needless to say, Hitler declared that war between Germany and Russia was henceforth unthinkable. Stalin doubtless did not take this quite at its face value, but he was not distressed by the prospect of the fascist and the democratic powers of central and western Europe tearing one another to pieces. He hoped to be the spectator of a prolonged and well-contested affair. The collapse of France in 1940, and the consequent reduction of Anglo-German warfare for several years to an affair of sideshows and air raids, upset his calculations.

Eight days of peace remained. On 25 August Hitler announced his determination to settle the Polish question in his own way, but at the same time offered to guarantee the security of the British Empire! He also suggested that, with Poland out of the way, the time would have come for a general reduction of armaments. But this time he discovered the truth of Lincoln's dictum, that you cannot fool all the people all the time. German troops invaded Poland on 1 September; Britain was at war with Germany at 11 a.m. on 3 September; France several hours later. This curious time-lag in the French declaration was symptomatic. For a year or more France had been dragged along, an unwilling somnambulist, at the heels of Great Britain. In 1939 the 'big three' of Europe were Chamberlain, Hitler, and Stalin. Mussolini was a rather bad fourth. Daladier, the French prime minister, was a nobody.

So the Germans once again, after an interval of twenty-five years and one month, entered on a great war of their own making. But the mood of 1939 was very different from the mood of 1914. In 1914 the whole population entered the war with exuberant optimism. They had fifty years of political and economic prosperity behind them. The second Reich never had been and never could be beaten. They had been looking forward to this for years. But in 1939 German memories included catastrophic defeat, political humiliation, and economic chaos. They had entrusted themselves to Hitler because they believed that he worked miracles and could secure them world power without a world war. They dreaded war. When the western democracies declared war on the Polish issue they were astonished, and they feared defeat from the first, though the mood doubtless passed off in 1940. This may not have been true of the Nazi youths in the fighting forces. It was almost certainly true of the civilians and the middle-aged. As for Hitler he very likely believed to the last that he would carry through the Polish business as peacefully as he had carried through the affairs of Czechoslovakia, Austria, the Rhineland and, most hazardous of all, his original rearmament. He had declared so long that the democracies were degenerate that he had very likely become the dupe of his own propaganda. It is the nemesis of inveterate liars that in the end they believe their own lies.

It is often said that the war of 1939–45 was an ideological war, fascism or tyranny against democracy or 'plutodemocracy'. But surely this is not so. Russia might have been in it from the first and was forced into it in 1941, and whatever Russia may be, she is not a democracy as the term is understood in western Europe and was understood in fifth-century Athens. The Russians described their enemies as

н

fascists, and themselves as communists, as though there were some profound ideological difference between these two things which to a democrat seem to bear a strong family likeness to one another. But Stalin's Russia was not even communist. Communism as Marx and Lenin understood it, had gone with the fall of the Trotskyites. Stalin was a nationalist dictator with a domestic programme of by no means 100 per cent socialism. Indeed he might be described as a National Socialist, which is 'longhand' for 'Nazi'. The difference between Hitler and Stalin was that Stalin had plenty of *Lebensraum* and Hitler had not. As for the smaller states occupied and terrorized by Hitler's armies in the course of the war, Belgium, Holland, Norway, Denmark, Hungary, Rumania, Bulgaria, Jugoslavia, Greece, some of them were democracies and others had for years past been ruled by dictators of the fascist pattern, but Hitler was no more interested in these ideological differences among his victims than a cannibal chief, feasting on missionary broth, would care whether the broth had once been a Roman Catholic or a Primitive Methodist.

No: the war was a war between the satisfied and the dissatisfied powers—to employ terms in common use during the period between the wars; and that at once raises the question whether the dissatisfactions of the dissatified were reasonable and could have been met. To take three small and concrete examples —in an ideally distributed world would 'Tunis! Nice! Corsica!' have belonged to France or to Italy, or perchance to neither? We do not propose to answer this question, but only to suggest that the answering of it is by no means easy, and also to remind the reader that the world is not ideally constituted. In an ideal world it would be doubtless reasonable that Germany should have been given a share of African colonial territory, but it would have been absurd in the world of the 1930s as she would at once have used such territories for military aerodromes and submarine harbours. On the whole it must be maintained that Germany could not have been given satisfaction, for her fundamental ground of dissatisfaction was the fact that she had been defeated in her first bid for world power, and was determined to make a second bid. As one reviews the history of the whole period from Armistice Day 1918 onwards, one is driven to the conclusion that nothing the victorious powers could have done, short of a complete obliteration of German independence, would have cured her of this determination. This alternative the victors of 1945 have imposed, with consequences which cannot be foreseen; in 1919 it was not within the scope or imagination of practical politics. None the less it remains true that, by their harsh treatment of her while she was weak and their complaint treatment of her when she became strong again, they made a bad prospect worse. If a hostile judgment is to be passed on the policy of Great Britain and France in relation to Germany during the period covered by this book, it should be that they reversed the advice given by Virgil to his Romans: *parcere subiectis et debellare superbos* (to spare the downtrodden and to beat down the proud).

V

THE FAR EAST

BUT little space remains for a record of that other stretch of history in which the central place is occupied not by Germany but by Japan, and it is perhaps as well to preface the record of events after 1918 by some paragraphs of introduction. We have presumed in the reader a general knowledge, sufficient for the purpose, of European history previous to the conclusion of the first great war, but it might be paying some of those who may read this book a compliment they neither desire nor deserve to assume that they possess an equally adequate recollection of events in the Far East.

Up to about a hundred years ago both China and Japan were virtually closed to all forms of European penetration. Then, by means of what is on the whole unfairly called the Opium War of 1838–40, Great Britain made a breach in the protective carapace of China, and fifteen years later Commodore Perry performed the same not altogether disinterested office for Japan. The reactions of China and Japan to these operations was different. As an American writer has neatly put it, the Opening of China meant that the Europeans went in and the Opening of Japan meant that the Japanese came out. China accepted grudgingly and unwillingly what was forcibly thrust upon her. Under compulsion she granted first to the British and afterwards to other European traders the lease of a variety of treaty ports, and within these ports the privileges of extra-territoriality, which means the right within them to administer their own laws. Outside these reluctantly granted concessions she hoped to continue to live her own life in her own way. Japan, after following for a few years the example of China, suddenly revolutionized her institutions and her ambitions and set herself to become, by imitation, a 'European' state. The Chinese despised European ways of life, and the Japanese flattered them by imitation, but it may be presumed that both Chinese and Japanese regarded, and regard, the European peoples themselves with equal detestation—and why not? We are troublesome intruders into their remote world. To-day Japan is the enemy and China, because she has more reason to fear the Japanese than us, the ally, but during the first half of the period covered by this book the hostility of the Chinese was a more conspicuous factor than the hostility of Japan.

Towards the end of the nineteenth century the situation in China looked rather like the situation in India a century and a half earlier. In China as in India various European powers, Great Britain foremost among them, had established a variety of coastal bases. Island Hong Kong might be paired off with island Bombay: Shanghai and Tientsin with Calcutta and Madras. The Manchu and the Mughal dynasties were both far gone in decay. A superficial observer might suppose that history would repeat itself and that an Anglo-Russian struggle for the control of all China would repeat the Anglo-French struggle for the control of all India. But in the Indian case there had been no Japan. The more Japan became Europeanized the more conscious she became of an imperial destiny. Apart from motives of prestige and ambition, her population had, ever since her revolution, been increasing prodigiously. Indeed to-day her population is, in relation to her cultivable area, the densest in the world. This population can only maintain its standard of living by the development of an increasing export trade, and in a world of high protective tariffs foreign markets are insecure without political control.

The obvious menace to Japan was from Russia, who had established her first Pacific port on territory wrested from China at Vladivostok in 1861, and began the building of the Trans-Siberian railway in 1885. If Russia got Korea, at that date a semi-independent apanage of China, she would occupy towards Japan a position like that of a Germany in possession of Belgium towards England. In 1894 Japan went to war with China over Korea. After a brief and victorious campaign she secured the 'independence' of Korea (which meant its control by herself), and also the Liaotung peninsula in southern Manchuria. Immediately after the conclusion of this treaty she was ordered out of Liaotung by a joint ultimation from Russia, France, and Germany. The Russian motive is obvious. France was Russia's new-found ally. Germany lent her powerful support because she felt that the more Russia was encouraged in the Far East, the less energy and ambition would she have left over for the Balkans, where her aims were in competition with those of Germany and Austria. Japan complied, and it was Russia, not Japan, who secured and developed the valuable harbour of Port Arthur at the tip of the Liaotung peninsula.

Japan's response was the Anglo-Japanese alliance of 1902. Great Britain was at that time, immediately after the South African War, very conscious of her isolation in a hostile world. She was also anxious to prevent the continuance of the southward drive of Russian imperialism in China. The main stipulation of the treaty was that if either party found itself at war with more than one great power, the other party would come to its assistance. Fortified by the Anglo-Japanese treaty and provoked by Russian interventions in Korea, Japan challenged Russia in 1904, completely defeated her at sea, and fought a series of successful battles against vast Russian armies in Manchuria. After eighteen months of war peace was arranged through the mediation of President Roosevelt, and the Liaotung peninsula returned once more to Japan.

The Russo-Japanese war was in all respects a great event of history. Japan definitely displaced Russia as the prospective conqueror of China, if China were one day to be conquered. Thus she became potentially the enemy of all those European powers which were anxious to preserve what was called 'the Open Door' in China, namely the right of all to compete freely and on a level of equal opportunity for Chinese markets. The most important powers in this category were Great Britain and America. None the less the Anglo-Japanese alliance was renewed after the Russo-Japanese war. As the German menace increased so did its value to Great Britain, for it enabled her to bring her Far Eastern Fleet back to home waters, leaving the protection of her interests in the Far East to Japan. For Russia her defeat meant a switching over of her ambitions once again from Manchuria to the Balkans, thus provoking the successive clashes with Austro-German ambitions which led up to the first great war. Finally, by establishing an oriental state as an equal of the great European powers in military prowess, the war gave an incalculable impulse to movements of opposition to European suzerainty in India and other oriental countries. How little that equality had been realized at the beginning of the war was illustrated by *Punch's* friendly but patronizing cartoon of 'Jap the Giant-killer'. The average Englishman's views about Japan had not yet got far beyond *The Mikado*—which for some years was banned from the English stage lest it should hurt the feelings of our ally.

The first great war automatically involved Japan by the terms of the Anglo-Japanese treaty, for Great Britain was at war with two great powers, Germany and Austria-Hungary. This suited Japan very well, for it gave her a perfectly correct pretext for seizing Tsingtao, a port on the Shantung peninsula which had been granted to Germany by China in 1898. The European war also opened up attractive opportunities for encroachment on China while rival encroachers had their hands full elsewhere. Hence the programme of the Twenty-one Demands presented in 1915, which would have established something like a Japanese protectorate over the Chinese Government. But diplomatic support from the United States stiffened Chinese resistance, and most of the demands were not granted in the Sino-Japanese treaty subsequently negotiated.

Japan was one of the three great naval powers at

the Washington Conference of 1922. Great Britain, the United States, and Japan agreed to limit the gross tonnage of their battleships, Japan's to be three-fifths of that of the other two powers. This might seem to place Japan in an inferior position, but as Japan's naval interests were confined to one ocean only it did not really do so, especially as Great Britain and America undertook to establish no naval bases at Hong Kong or the Philippines. Great Britain's naval power in the Far East was henceforth to be based on Singapore, and America's on Pearl Harbour in Hawaii, the former more than 3,000 and the latter more than 4,000 miles from Tokyo.

Another result of the Washington Conference was the termination of the Anglo-Japanese alliance. Japan desired its continuance, and so did we so far as our own immediate interests were concerned. We decided to sacrifice it and incur the ill-will of Japan because it was obnoxious to the Dominions and still more to the United States. It was replaced by a four-power pact in which Great Britain, America, Japan, and China each undertook to respect each others *island* possessions in the Far East, and also by a nine-power pact which was a sort of local League of Nations Covenant embracing all the states which had a stake, large or small, in Far Eastern affairs. The abandonment of the Anglo-Japanese alliance at this juncture may have been a mistake; it certainly failed to secure any noticeable manifestations of goodwill from America in the ensuing years.

We must now go back eleven years and take up the course of events in China from the date of the

Chinese revolution of 1911. Previous to that date, for over two thousand years, the constitution of China had remained virtually unchanged, even though power had on various occasions been violently transferred from one ruling dynasty to another. The rule of the emperor was in theory autocratic, but in practice his control over the provinces was confined to the appointment of governors and the requisitioning from them of funds to meet the central expenditure. In fact the empire was in essentials a loose federation, its only bond of union being a traditional veneration of the emperor. The Manchus, who had ruled for the past two hundred years, had been foreign conquerors from a semi-barbaric province outside the tradional limits of Chinese civilization, like the Mongol Khans whom Marco Polo had visited and described six hundred years before. Even in China dynasties do not last for ever, and the Manchu régime might in any case have declined and fallen at this time, but the character of its decline and of the régime which replaced it were coloured by the infiltration of revolutionary European ideas. The revolution of 1911 was not merely a change of dynasty; it was the establishment of what purported to be a parliamentary republic in a country with a population more than three times as large as the United States, 99 per cent of whom were illiterate. Of all the imitations of the British constitution which have been launched upon the world since the days of the French Constituent Assembly of 1789, this was the most enormous and the most absurd.

The authors of the revolution were the westernized intellectuals of Canton who took their lead from the

philosopher Sun Yat-sen. They called themselves
Kuomintang, the National party. Sun, however,
refused the presidency and pressed it upon Yuan
Shih-kai, a conservative soldier, who quickly got
rid of his parliamentary encumbrances, became a
dictator, tried to found a new imperial dynasty,
failed, and died in 1916. Henceforth, for a period of
fourteen years China was in a state of civil war
between rival Tuchuns, or provincial governors
turned bandits. While the population of India was
multiplying at an enormous rate under the crushing
yoke of British 'tyranny', the population of China
was being reduced with at least equal rapidity under
the stimulus of 'liberty'.

Among the parties to the civil war was the Canton
Kuomintang, and Sun Yat-sen came under the
influence of a Communist emissary from Soviet
Russia, named Borodin. In 1925 Sun died, and
Borodin, who had observed the unifying influence of
Lenin-worship in his own country, had Sun's body,
like Lenin's, embalmed. A cult in his honour was
propagated and his writings elevated to the rank of
scriptures. Thus an impracticable and disastrous
politician was converted into a very potent 'saint'.[1]
Thus also Russia, driven back from the northern end
of China by the Japanese military pitchfork in 1905,
reinserted herself as an ideology at the southern end
of China twenty years later. Indeed it might have
been supposed at this time, as Mr. Gathorne-Hardy
remarks in his excellent *History of International*

---

[1] History furnishes many parallels, that of St. Thomas
(Becket) of Canterbury, being the first that comes to my mind;
but the transformation in this case was spontaneous, not
designed by a twelfth-century Borodin.

Affairs 1920–39, that Kuomintang was a Chinese transliteration of Comintern, the name of the Russian Communist propaganda department. Under Russian influence industrial disturbances were organized in the international settlements in Shanghai and Canton, and a demand for the abolition of the extra-territorial privileges of Europeans was raised. This was in 1925. In 1927 there were similar troubles at Hankow and Kiukiang.

Meanwhile, however, a new figure had arisen within the Kuomintang party, General Chiang Kai-shek, who fortified his position by marrying the sister of the widow of Sun Yat-sen. He gradually succeeded in extruding the Russian and communist influences from the party. The Chinese communist party survived, however, and survives (1945) as a powerful organization, separate from and hostile to the authority of Chiang Kai-shek. While Chiang was establishing his authority within the Kuomintang he was also conducting a series of successful campaigns against the rival Tuchuns. By 1930 he had established his authority over the greater part of China, and had entered on negotiations with the British Labour Government for the abolition of the extraterritorial privileges in the 'Concession' cities, negotiations which were regarded with some alarm by the Far Eastern trading corporations who would be principally affected. Mr. Justice Feetham, an eminent South African lawyer, who had originally gone to South Africa as one of Milner's 'young men', invited to report on the problem, expressed the opinion that, while abolition was in the long run inevitable, an immediate abolition would be disastrous, and that a transitional system would be required for 'not years but decades'. However, the progress of this controversy was interrupted by an intrusion from Japan.

Japan, like other countries dependent on export trade, had been seriously affected by the great slump. In particular, the slump in America had ruined one of her principal export trades, that of raw silk to the United States. In these circumstances Japanese attention concentrated on Manchuria, the large and rich province which constituted the hinterland of the Liaotung peninsula. Japan had secured a variety of treaty rights in Manchuria both after the Russo-Japanese war and during the first great war, and these rights had been constantly infringed by various Chinese rulers during the period of Chinese anarchy. To-day we naturally incline to condemn the whole of the policy of aggressive imperialism pursued by Japan from 1931 onwards, but the course of action pursued was, in its first phases, not very different from that pursued by many European empires, including our own, when confronted with similar circumstances. In the winter of 1931–2 Japanese armies invaded and occupied southern Manchuria, and converted it into an 'independent' empire of Manchukuo under a puppet who was the heir of the dethroned Manchu dynasty. At the same time, as a reply to anti-Japanese demonstrations, Japanese forces bombarded Shanghai, and thereby interrupted the opening of the European Disarmament Conference.

China had, some months earlier, appealed to the League of Nations for protection against Japan, and the case was at once accepted, like the Abyssinian case already described (though it occurred four years

later), as a test case for the practicability of the
League organization for the prevention of aggression.
As in the Abyssinian case it was quickly apparent
that League action would mean British action, no
other member being able or willing to do anything
that was likely to impress Japan. America associated
herself as an 'observer' with the League discussions,
but the only positive contribution of American statesmanship was the 'doctrine of non-recognition', on
which Mr. Gathorne-Hardy dryly remarks that
'history lends little support to the idea that non-
recognition of a *de facto* situation can be permanently
maintained'. On the industrial side America made a
much more positive contribution; her industrialists
then and for years afterwards furnished the Japanese
with most of their imported munitions. Much of
China's munitions came, oddly enough, from
Germany.

As a means of postponing decision the Japanese
suggested the appointment of an international commission of inquiry to discover the facts on the spot.
Such a commission was appointed under the chairmanship of Lord Lytton. The commission condemned
Japanese aggression and offered a series of proposals
involving international co-operation which would
secure the rights of both China and Japan. Nothing
came of this. Early in 1933 Japan renounced her
membership of the League, resumed her westward
advance and occupied the province of Jehol, which
brought her to the gates of Peiping (Peking).
Chiang removed the headquarters of his government
to Nanking on the Yangtse-kiang. In 1934 Japan
denounced the Washington naval treaty, and in
1936 allied herself with Germany in the so-called

Anti-Comintern Pact. It was the year of the Berlin-Rome Axis. The three 'dissatisfied' great powers were drawing together.

It would be impossible without entering on an examination of the complicated internal politics of Japan to say at what precise moment the policy of limited aggression in Manchuria, which had for forty years been a bone of contention between China, Russia, and Japan, was superseded in the minds of the Japanese ruling cliques, military and naval, political and commercial, by grandiose schemes of a 'new order' of the whole Far Eastern area of the world, in which not only all China but also Siam, Malaya, Burma and the whole of the East Indies should become tributary provinces of a Japanese Empire. Such schemes had long been discussed and applauded in unofficial circles. The Japanese regarded themselves as the equivalent of a European 'great power'. If the British had conquered an incorrigibly disorderly and anarchical India—for its own good, as the British so often maintained—why should not the Japanese do the same with an incorrigibly disorderly and anarchical China? If the British held island bases all over the world, why should not the Japanese hold island bases all over the western Pacific? True, Java and other islands had already been pre-empted by the Dutch, the Philippines by America, New Guinea by Australia, but prizes that had fallen to one empire might be wrested from it by the might of a rival; and if one empire had more right than another to these prizes, surely that right belonged to the only great power whose homeland was located in the Far East. The Japanese regarded themselves as the *Herrenvolk*, the master race, of the Far East and all Far Eastern territories as their legitimate *Lebensraum.*

The launching of the new policy of unlimited aggression, so far as China was concerned, was precipitated by an agreement of December 1936, which opened up prospects, eventually unfulfilled, of a reconciliation between Kuomintang and the Chinese communists. If Chiang Kai-shek were really about to become the effective ruler of all China, the Japanese onslaught ought not to be delayed until that prospect had become a reality. In the course of 1937–8 Japanese armies occupied such great and widely dispersed cities as Peking, Shanghai, Nanking, Canton, and Hankow. Chiang's Government withdrew a thousand miles up the Yangtse-kiang to Chungking, which was subjected to Japanese bombardment from the air. But victory was not in sight. Chiang showed no signs of any intention to abandon the struggle, and the conquest in a single war of so vast an area as China began to look like an impossibility. In 1939 a Japanese attempt to seize Changsha, in Human, one of the chief 'rice bowls' of China, proved a complete failure, and an invasion of northern Manchuria was repulsed with heavy losses by the Russians.

The Russo-German neutrality pact of August 1939 came as a serious blow to Japan who had imagined that the anti-comintern pact had meant what it said. However, the defeat of France in the summer of 1940, soon to be followed, as they like most of the rest of the world outside the British Empire expected, by the conquest of Britain, brightened Japanese prospects in other directions. France and Britain were both persuaded by force of circumstances to cut off their supplies to China, Britain by the closing for three months of the Burma Road, and France by stopping exports from Indo-China. In April 1941, when the German invasion of Russia was imminent, Russia agreed to a neutrality pact with Japan. In July the Vichy Government of France surrendered Indo-China to Japanese occupation, which enabled Japanese armies to concentrate on the frontier of Burma. In the same month General Tojo, the leader of the extreme imperialists, entered the Cabinet as Minister of War. In November the Japanese Government sent a special envoy to the United States to discuss, among other things, the embargo on the export of oil to Japan which the American Government had imposed in the previous year. It was during the progress of these negotiations, intended, no doubt, to foster in America a false sense of security, that Japanese carrier-borne aircraft attempted to put out of action before war began the most formidable fleet that could be brought into action against them by the attack on Pearl Harbour, Honolulu, on 7 December. On the same day air attacks were delivered on Manila, Shanghai, Hong Kong, and Singapore.

The great Japanese gamble, cradled in treachery, had begun. It was really a very foolish gamble. Hitler's chances of conquering Britain had obviously declined from their peak in the autumn of the previous year, and in spite of his initial successes there was no convincing evidence that he could conquer Russia. The resources of America were intact and immeasurable. In the long run the resources of the coalition that Japan was provoking were immeasurably greater than her own. But the

Japanese Government, like the German Government, were probably the victims of their own propaganda. Like the Germans they had long been insufferably conceited, and their bid for the domination of the Far East, like the German bid for world power everywhere else, was not only very wicked but also, as they would find out in due course, a very stupid undertaking.

APPENDIX I

President Wilson's Fourteen Points, Four Principles, and Five Particulars

The Fourteen Points (speech of 8 January, 1918).

1. Open covenants openly arrived at, after which there shall be no private international understandings of any kind, but diplomacy shall proceed always frankly and in public view.

2. Absolute freedom of navigation upon the seas outside territorial waters alike in peace and war, except as the seas may be closed in whole or in part by international action for the enforcement of international covenants.

3. The removal as far as possible of all economic barriers and the establishment of an equality of trade conditions among all the nations consenting to the peace and associating themselves for its maintenance.

4. Adequate guarantees given and taken that national armaments will be reduced to the lowest point consistent with domestic safety.

5. A free, open-minded and absolutely impartial adjustment of all colonial claims based upon a strict observance of the principle that in determining such questions of sovereignty the interests of the populations concerned must have equal weight with the equitable claims of the government whose title is to be determined.

6. The evacuation of all Russian territory, and such a settlement of all questions affecting Russia as will secure the best and free-est co-operation of the other nations of the world in obtaining for her an unhampered and unembarrassed opportunity for the independent determination of her own political development and national policy, and assure her a sincere welcome into the society of free nations under institutions of her own choosing,

and more than a welcome, assistance also of every kind that she may need and may herself desire. The treatment accorded to Russia by her sister nations in the months to come will be the acid test of their goodwill, of their comprehension of her needs as distinguished from their own interests, and of their intelligent and unselfish sympathy.

7. Belgium, the whole world will agree, must be evacuated and restored without any attempt to limit the sovereignty which she enjoys in common with other free nations.

8. All French territory should be freed and the invaded portions restored, and the wrong done to France by Prussia in 1871 in the matter of Alsace-Lorraine, which has unsettled the peace of the world for nearly fifty years, should be righted.

9. A readjustment of the frontiers of Italy should be effected along clearly recognizable lines of nationality.

10. The peoples of Austria-Hungary, whose place among the nations we wish to see safeguarded and assured, should be accorded the free-est opportunity of autonomous development.

11. Rumania, Serbia, and Montenegro should be evacuated, occupied territories restored, Serbia accorded free and secure access to the sea, and the relations of the several Balkan States to one another determined by friendly counsel along historically established lines of allegiance and nationality.

12. The Turkish portions of the present Ottoman Empire should be assured a secure sovereignty, but the other nationalities that are now under Turkish rule should be assured an undoubted security of life and an unmolested opportunity of autonomous development, and the Dardanelles should be permanently opened as a free passage to the ships and commerce of all nations, under international guarantees.

13. An independent Polish State should be created which should include the territories inhabited by

indisputably Polish populations, which should be assured a free and secure access to the sea, and whose political and economic independence should be guaranteed by international covenant.

14. A general association of nations should be formed under specific covenants for the purpose of affording mutual guarantees of political independence and territorial integrity to great and small states alike.

The Four Principles (speech of 11 February 1918).

1. That each part of the final settlement must be based on the essential justice of that particular case and upon such adjustments as are most likely to bring a peace that is permanent.

2. That peoples and provinces are not to be bartered about from sovereignty to sovereignty, as if they were chattels or pawns in a game, even the great game, now for ever discredited, of the balance of power; but that

3. Every territorial settlement involved in this war must be made in the interest and for the benefit of the populations concerned, and not as a part of any mere adjustment or compromise of claims among rival states; and

4. That all well-defined national aspirations shall be accorded that utmost satisfaction that can be accorded them without introducing new or perpetuating old elements of discord and antagonism that would be likely in time to break the peace of Europe and consequently of the world.

The Five Particulars (speech of 27 September 1918).

1. The impartial justice meted out must involve no distinction between those to whom we wish to be just and those to whom we do not wish to be just. It must be a justice that plays no favourites and knows no standards but the equal rights of the several peoples concerned.

2. No special or separate interest of any single nation or any group of nations can be made the basis of any part of the settlement which is not consistent with the common interest of all.

3. There can be no leagues or alliances or special covenants and understandings within the general and common family of the League of Nations.

4. And, more specifically, there can be no special selfish economic combinations within the League and no employment of any form of economic boycott or exclusion, except as the power of economic penalty, by exclusion from the markets of the world, may be vested in the League of Nations itself as a means of discipline and control.

5. All international agreements and treaties of every kind must be made known in their entirety to the rest of the world. Special alliances and economic rivalries and hostilities have been the prolific source in the modern world of the plans and passions that produce war. It would be an insincere as well as an insecure peace that did not exclude them in definite and binding terms.

APPENDIX II

The Covenant of the League of Nations

The Covenant constitutes the first chapter of the Treaty of Versailles. It is too long to be given in full here. The following is a summary of its twenty-six articles with some notes thereon, which are placed in brackets. Sentences between inverted commas give the actual words of the document.

1. Membership of the League is confined to the forty-two self-governing states and dominions mentioned by name and such others as may be afterwards elected by a two-thirds majority of the Assembly. Members may withdraw from the League on giving two years' notice.

2. The League shall act by means of an Assembly, a Council, and a Secretariat.

3. In the Assembly each member may have three representatives but only one vote. It may deal with any matter affecting the peace or welfare of the world in general. [It usually met once a year.]

4. The Council was to consist of representatives of Great Britain, France, Italy, Japan, and the United States [which refused to join. At later dates Germany and Russia were admitted.] These were permanent members. There was also to be four temporary member states [from 1925 onwards, six], elected by the Assembly from time to time at its discretion. Any other state might send a representative when matters were to be discussed which specially affected its interests. [The Council met three or four times a year.]

5. Except on matters of procedure, all decisions of the Council and the Assembly required a unanimous vote, except where otherwise specified in the Covenant.

6. The Secretariat shall consist of a Secretary-General and such staff as he may require. Sir Eric Drummond,

of the British Foreign Office, to be the first Secretary-General. [The staff was, so far as possible, recruited from citizens of all the states in the League.]

7. Geneva to be the headquarters of the League.

8. Plans to be drafted by the Council for the general reduction of armaments. Members of the League undertake to exchange full and frank information as to their military, naval, and air programmes.

9. A permanent advisory commission on armaments to be established.

10. 'Members of the League undertake to respect and preserve as against external aggression the territorial integrity and existing political independence of all members of the League. In case of any such aggression or of any threat or danger of such aggression the Council shall advise upon the means by which this obligation shall be fulfilled.'

11. 'Any war or threat of war . . . is hereby declared a matter of concern to the whole League, and the League shall take any action that may be deemed wise and effectual to safeguard the peace of nations. In case any such emergency should arise the Secretary-General shall on the request of any member of the League forthwith summon a meeting of the Council.'

12. 'The members of the League agree that if there should arise between them any dispute likely to lead to a rupture they will submit the matter either to arbitration *or to judicial settlement* or to inquiry by the Council and they agree in no case to resort to war until three months after the award of the arbitrators *or the judicial decision* or the report of the Council.' [The words in italics were added in 1924 after the establishment of the International Court at The Hague.]

13. Types of dispute appropriate for each of the above methods of settlement are described.

14. Arrangements for the subsequent establishment of the Court of International Justice. [Established 1921.]

15. The Council is to inquire into all disputes not otherwise settled, and to endeavour to bring the parties to agreement. If it fails to bring them to agreement it is to publish a report on the merits of the case. If its report is unanimous except for the votes of the parties to the dispute, members agree not to go to war with any state that accepts the award.

16. 'Should any member of the League resort to war in disregard of its covenants under articles 12, 13, or 15 it shall *ipso facto* be deemed to have committed an act of war against all other members of the League, which hereby undertake immediately to subject it to the severance of all trade and financial relations, the prohibition of all intercourse between their nationals and the nationals of the covenant-breaking state. . . . It shall be the duty of the Council in such a case to recommend to the several governments concerned what effective naval, military, or air force the members of the League shall contribute to the armed forces to be used to protect the covenants of the League.' [This is the article applied very incompletely and half-heartedly to Italy when she invaded Abyssinia. See page 162.]

17. Provisions regarding disputes between members of the League and states which are not members. Such states are to be invited to make use of the facilities of the League provided in articles 12–15, and if they refuse they are to be treated as in article 16.

18. No treaty to be binding unless registered with the League.

19. The Assembly is invited to 'advise' the reconsideration of such treaties as may be out of date. [Since such 'advice' had to be unanimous it was not likely to be offered.   One weakness of the League was that it possessed, on paper, great powers for preserving the *status quo* and very little power for making such alterations as the passage of time might require.]

20. No obligations inconsistent with the Covenant

[e.g. alliances of the old type] are to remain binding on members of the League. [For example, Hitler claimed that the Franco-Russian treaty of 1935 was inconsistent with the obligations of the Covenant, but in fact it had been carefully framed so as to be consistent with those obligations. Germany had already renounced her membership of the League at the time, so that Hitler's plea is a curious example of 'the devil quoting Scripture'.]

21. Other international obligations continue to be valid, for example the American 'Monroe Doctrine' specifically mentioned in this clause. [This clause was inserted to placate America. The Monroe Doctrine roughly means 'U.S.A. will not intervene in Europe and Europe must not intervene in the affairs of North or South America'. It is difficult to see how this Doctrine could be reconciled with the obligations of the Covenant.]

22. Provision for the disposal of the former colonies of Germany and the provinces detached from the Turkish Empire, i.e. the Mandates system [see page 68].

23. Other duties to be undertaken by the League. These include the improvement of industrial conditions [for which an International Labour Office independent of the League, but also operating in Geneva, was established], supervision of international trade in materials of war, extirpation of the 'white slave traffic' and the traffic in opium and other dangerous drugs.

24. All international organizations already existing are to be placed under the direction of the League.

25. Members of the League undertake to support the Red Cross and similar voluntary international organizations.

26. The Covenant can be amended by a unanimous vote of the Council together with a majority vote of the Assembly.

BIBLIOGRAPHY

ANYTHING like a complete bibliography of the subject is impossible here. The following are a few suggestions for further reading:

Gathorne-Hardy, G. M.: *A Short History of International Affairs*, 1920–39.

Nicolson, Harold, *Peacemaking.*

Butler, Harold, *The Lost Peace.*

Bryant, Arthur, *Unfinished Victory.*

Schwartzchild, Leopold, *World in Trance.*

Brogan, D. M., *The Development of Modern France, 1870–1939.*

Frazer, Lindley, *Germany between the Wars.*

Butler, R. d'O., *Roots of National Socialism.*

Jordan W. M., *Great Britain, France and the German Problem.*

Ludwig, Emil, *Hindenburg and the Saga of the German Revolution.*

Nevins, Allan, *America and World Affairs.*

Hudson, G. F., *The Far East in World Politics.*

INDEX

The so-called Great Powers are not included in this Index.

Printed by Jarrold & Sons Ltd., The Empire Press, Norwich